Discover the Magic of your Microwave

Discover the Magic of your Microwave

Chrissie Taylor

W. FOULSHAM AND CO. LTD.

London • New York • Toronto • Cape Town • Sydney

W. Foulsham & Company Limited
Bennetts Close, Cippenham, Berkshire, SL1 5AP

ISBN 0–572–02378–2

Originally published under the title *Reveal the Magic
of the Microwave*

Printed in Great Britain by St Edmundsbury Press Limited
Bury St Edmunds, Suffolk

PREFACE

Even before qualifying as a Home Economist at Westminster Technical College in 1972 it was my ambition to write a book related to my most loved passion – catering. I have always enjoyed inventing recipes, putting ideas into action and giving my cookery appliances a special place in my kitchen. When I became a microwave owner three years ago it was a challenge to discover its powers beyond being a time-saver and cutting down on the washing-up.

I now have discovered some of its magic powers and I take this opportunity to share them with you. So many microwave books only give recipes. I hope this book will teach you much more and reveal the hidden potential of the 'Magic Box' which deserves a special place in the 20th-century kitchen. My microwave has become more than an appliance – it is an essential friend in the the fast-moving world in which we live.

Thanks to Mum, Dad, Liz and Chris for their encouragement. To Bruce for his understanding and support in writing this book.

For my daughter Sophie with love

CONTENTS

USEFUL INFORMATION

* All the processes and recipes in this publication have been tested by the author using a 700 watt microwave cooker. It is essential that the directions are followed precisely and that all of the manufacturer's instructions are strictly adhered to. The author can accept no responsibility for the outcome should the user fail to do this.

* The Ministry of Agriculture, Fisheries and Food have issued a statement explaining that as they cannot provide an accurate answer as to what degree Clingfilm is harmful in a microwave cooker, the use of clingfilm should be left to the discretion of the user.

In future, clingfilm that does contain the harmful DEHA plasticiser, used to make clingfilm stretchy, will state what the film can be used for. If there are no instructions, it should not be used for microwave cooking.

Examples of clingfilm that do not contain the DEHA plasticiser are Purecling and Saran Wrap. Roast-a-bags are also safe to use.

* For very short cooking times, if you do not have a digital timer on your microwave cooker, check the timing by using the second hand of a watch, timer or clock.

* It is important that either metric or imperial measures are followed in all recipes, not a combination of both.

* Spoon measures
1 level tablespoon – 15 ml
1 level teaspoon – 5 ml
Spoon measurements in all recipes are level.

* When herbs are used in a recipe, the flavour of dried is stronger than fresh, so use half the quantity of dried. (Unless stated otherwise, dried herbs are used in all the recipes in this book.)

TEN TEMPTING THOUGHTS

1. Washing-up is cut to a minimum as many foods can be prepared and served in the same dish.

2. Individual tastes are catered for in much less time.

3. There is no need for waste when owning a microwave as reheating of leftovers is so easy and there is only minimal loss of flavour.

4. When cooking whole cuts of meat, e.g. chops, steaks, joints, poultry, there is less shrinkage.

5. Vegetables retain more of their nutrients and have a better texture than when conventionally cooked as less water is used.

6. Slightly stale or soft foods can be refreshed or re-crisped in the microwave, e.g., cereals, bread, coffee beans, etc.

7. Warm plates in the microwave, with a small jug of water to absorb some of the microwave energy – it saves turning the oven on!

8. Heat baby bottles and food quickly and without fuss at odd hours.

9. The microwave is so versatile it can be wheeled on a trolley into the garden to warm rolls, drinks and half cook food for barbecues.

10. Dry flowers between sheets of kitchen paper, to preserve their beautiful appearance. Remember to place a glass of water in the cooker before microwaving.

TEN BASIC TIPS

1. Food cooked dry or with very little liquid, e.g. whole fish or chicken portions, should be placed in a dish relative to their size and with a well-fitting lid to retain moisture.

2. Never cook high fat or sugar content foods in plastic containers unless recommended by the manufacturers.

3. Place thinner parts of food towards the centre of the dish, thicker and more dense pieces towards the outside.

4. Bone in meat conducts heat, so cooking the meat next to the bone first. A boneless cut of meat cooks much more evenly, so whenever possible remove bones.

5. Stir soups, sauces and casseroles during cooking to ensure an even distribution of heat. If stirring food is impossible, rotate the dish two or three times during cooking.

6. Cut ingredients into equal-sized pieces when microwaving casseroles to ensure even cooking.

7. Always stand or rest food after microwaving to complete cooking and equalize the temperature throughout the food. When in doubt always undercook.

8. Occasionally sparking may occur, when small amounts of food are microwaved. Stop the cooker immediately and place a small cup of water in the cooker with the food. Some of the microwave energy will be transferred to heat the water and cooking can be continued safely.

9. Food taken from the refrigerator will take longer to cook than that at room temperature, especially during the summer or warm weather.

10. Follow your nose: when you begin to smell the food cooking it has probably had sufficient time in the microwave.

TEN REHEATING RULES

1. Always pierce clingfilm or roll back at one edge, otherwise it will explode.

2. Place thinner parts of food towards the centre of the dish and cover with gravy or sauce if possible to ensure that they do not dry out.

3. Cover food to be reheated with vented or pierced clingfilm, kitchen paper, greaseproof paper or a microwave lid according to the type of food to be reheated.

4. Dishes containing one ingredient will reheat more evenly than a combination of foods.

5. To reheat an average meal, cover with pierced clingfilm, plate or microwave lid and cook on 100% High for 3 – 3½ minutes. For more than one meal add approximately 1½ minutes to the cooking time.

6. Never reheat more than two plates of food sitting directly on top of each other, as the air passage will be restricted. Use microwave plate stacking rings for safety and do not reheat more than three meals at a time.

7. After reheating, place your hand underneath the centre of the plate or dish: if it is hot, the food is fully reheated.

8. Rotate dishes or plates of food during reheating to distribute the heat evenly.

9. Stir or toss food where possible during reheating to distribute the heat evenly, e.g. warming casseroles or stews, custards, sauces, soups, vegetables, etc.

10. Fruit and vegetables will reheat more quickly and retain moisture if they are three-quarter covered.

CONVENTIONAL RECIPE CONVERSION

Many conventional recipes can be cooked in the microwave. The most difficult factor in their success is judging the correct timing. As a guide:

1. Reduce the cooking time to a quarter of the conventional cooking time when using 100% High power level.

2. Reduce the cooking time by half when using 50% Medium power level.

3. Reduce the cooking time to three-quarters of the conventional cooking time when using Low (Defrost).

4. Add more thickening agent or reduce the liquid by a quarter especially when cooking casseroles.

Other factors to help in your recipe conversions are listed throughout the A – Z book, e.g. cakes, seasonings, fruit juice in crumbles, etc.

Remember to make a note of the quantities used, the power level and the cooking time so that you do not have to convert the recipe again.

REDUCING/INCREASING MICROWAVE RECIPES

As in conventional recipe conversion, the most difficult factor when reducing or increasing a recipe is the timing.

REDUCING

1. Choose a smaller dish.

2. If halving a recipe, microwave for approximately two-thirds of the original time. If quartering, microwave for approximately one-third of the original time.

3. Check food to see if cooked before end of calculated cooking time. Overcooked food cannot be rectified.

4. Reduce the standing time accordingly.

5. Do not reduce recipes with a high fat and sugar content as they will burn.

6. If microwaving very small amounts of food, e.g. chocolate, place a small glass of water in the cooker to absorb some of the microwave energy.

INCREASING

1. When increasing a recipe by one-half, increase the cooking time by one-third.

2. When doubling a recipe, increase the cooking time by one-half.

3. Place the food in a larger dish.

4. Increase the standing time accordingly.

5. Check food to see if it is cooked before the end of the calculated cooking time.

MICROWAVE POWER CONVERSION

All the recipes and tips in this book have been tried and tested using a 700 watt microwave cooker.

For a 600 watt microwave add 20 seconds per minute to the cooking time when using fresh ingredients.

For a 500 watt microwave add 40 seconds per minute to the cooking time when using fresh ingredients.

When reheating cooked or tinned foods add a few seconds to the total time for all the lower wattage cookers. Recipes and tips using 50% Medium power level are best cooked on 100% High for slightly less time if you do not own a variable power microwave. To adapt the timings to a lower wattage cooker, use the following table:

TIMING

650/700 watt		600 watt		500 watt	
Mins	Secs	Mins	Secs	Mins	Secs
	15		20		25
	45	1	–	1	15
1	–	1	20	1	40
2	–	2	40	3	20
3	–	4	–	5	–
4	–	5	20	6	40
5	–	6	40	8	20
6	–	8	–	10	–
7	–	9	20	11	40
8	–	10	40	13	20
9	–	12	–	15	–
10	–	13	20	16	40

A

ALMONDS

BLANCHING

Pour 225 ml (8 fl oz) boiling water over 125 g (4 oz) whole almonds in their skins. Microwave uncovered on 100% High for 1 minute. Drain and cool slightly. The skins can then be removed by squeezing each nut between the finger and thumb. Spread on kitchen paper and leave to dry.

TOASTING

Place 125 g (4 oz) skinned almonds (whole or split) in a dish with 25 g (1 oz) butter. Cover and microwave on 100% High for 2 minutes, tossing frequently to result in even browning.

APPLES

Dessert and cooking apples are cooked successfully in the microwave. Stewed and baked apples maintain their shape and colour well and need little or no additional liquid due to the high water content of the fruit.

BAKED

Wash, dry and core the fruit. Pierce the skin a few times with a fork or score round the centre. Place in a round casserole dish and stuff the middle of each apple with filling. Cover and microwave on 100% High. Four apples will take 7–9 minutes, depending on their size. Leave to stand for 5 minutes, spoon over juices and serve with custard or whipped cream.

For fillings, choose one of the following:

Mincemeat   Ready-made mincemeat is ideal and timesaving. Use 1 tbsp for each apple.

Orange   Mix together 1 tbsp each of chopped nuts, brown sugar, sultanas, currants, desiccated coconut. Bind with the grated rind and juice of 1 orange.

Spiced   Mix together 1 tbsp each of brown sugar, sultanas and chopped dates with ½ tsp nutmeg or mixed spice. Bind with the grated rind and juice of 1 lemon.

SAUCE

To make a speedy apple sauce, peel, core and chop 450 g (1 lb) fruit and place in a bowl with 15 g (½ oz) unsalted butter or margarine and ¼ tsp ground cloves. Cover and microwave on 100% High for 8 minutes. Mash to a pulp and serve hot or cold as an accompaniment to pork, e.g. roast, chops, steaks, sausages, escalopes. The cloves may be omitted and the skin left on the apples if preferred.

STEWED

Choose unblemished and firm fruit. A crisp apple is more suitable for pie filling as the slices hold their shape better. Peel, core and slice 450 g (1 lb) fruit evenly and place in a deep dish.

Mix together 75 g (3 oz) granulated or brown sugar with 2 tbsp water, 1 tbsp lemon juice and 1 tsp spice of your choice, e.g. nutmeg, cinnamon, mixed spice.

Spread over apples and toss to coat well. Cover and microwave on 100% High for 6–8 minutes, stirring once halfway through cooking time. Leave to stand for 2 minutes before serving. If the stewed apple is for pie filling, uncover after cooking and leave to cool. If stewing dessert apples, reduce the amount of sugar accordingly.

APRICOTS

DRIED

It is not necessary to soak dried apricots overnight before cooking them in the microwave, although soaking achieves a slightly better result. Place 225 g (8 oz) in a bowl with 600 ml (1 pt) water. Cover with a lid and microwave on 100% High for 15 minutes, stirring once during cooking. Leave to stand for 10 minutes and use as required.

For a more interesting flavour substitute unsweetened fruit juice for half the water. Thicken any remaining juice with cornflour, sweeten with sugar and use as a sauce for puddings, sponges, ice-cream and fruit.

PEELING

Microwave each fresh apricot for 5–10 seconds on 100% High. Stand for 30 seconds before removing the skin.

POACHING

Pierce skins or prick with a fork to prevent them from bursting if cooking whole. Place 450 g (1 lb) fruit in a bowl with 1 tbsp water and microwave on 100% High for 3–4 minutes. Stir once during cooking if the fruit is stoned and halved. Stand for 3 minutes. Serve hot with a liqueur syrup sauce, blanched almonds or fresh cream.

If using to fill flans, poach the apricots whole to retain their shape. Cool, halve and remove stones.

PURÉEING

Cook as if poaching. When cool, place the fruit in a liquidizer or food processor with enough sugar syrup to give a thick pouring consistency. Serve as a sauce for ice-cream, sweet puddings and sponges or as an accompaniment for gammon and bacon.

See *Sugar Syrup*

ASPARAGUS

Fresh asparagus cooks so much better in a microwave than when conventionally cooked. As so little water is used, its rich colour is maintained and the full flavour of the vegetable can be appreciated.

Choose stalks of similar thickness and length if possible, so that they will cook evenly. Trim the ends off 450 g (1 lb) and arrange the stalks in a shallow dish with the spears pointing towards the centre. Sprinkle with 2–4 tbsp water, cover with pierced clingfilm and microwave on 100% High for 6–7 minutes until just tender but crisp. Stand for 2 minutes. Drain and serve with a glaze of melted butter or lemon butter and a garnish of lemon slices. Sprinkle with sesame seeds or blanched split almonds.

See *Butter*, *Flavoured*, and *Almonds*

AUBERGINES

Aubergines are cooked quickly in the microwave without any risk of discoloration.

SLICES

Cook aubergine for moussaka by placing 450 g (1 lb) slices in a casserole with 4 tbsp boiling water. Cover with pierced clingfilm and microwave on 100% High for 6–8 minutes, tossing twice during cooking. Stand for 3 minutes.

Microwave a prepared moussaka to serve four on 100% High for 10–12 minutes, turning the dish once during cooking. Stand for 3 minutes. Brown under a hot grill or garnish with sliced tomato and parsley.

WHOLE

Wash and trim the ends of 450g (1 lb) aubergines. Prick the skins and brush with oil. Place on a sheet of kitchen paper and microwave on 100% High for 4–5 minutes, rearranging and turning once during cooking. Stand for 3 minutes.

The aubergines are ready to use in your favourite stuffed aubergine recipe. After filling, arrange in a dish, cover and microwave on 100% High for 6–7 minutes, turning once during cooking. Stand for 3 minutes and serve with tomato sauce if liked.

See *Sauces*, *Tomato*

B

BABIES' FOOD

BOTTLES

Babies bottles cannot be sterilized using a microwave cooker. Use a proprietary sterilizing agent for their specialized care.

JARS

Remove metal caps, cover loosely with clingfilm and microwave on 100% High for 15–30 seconds. Stir and serve straight from the jar.

MILK

Heat 200 ml (7 fl oz) milk in a sterilized baby's bottle (teat and covering cap may be left on) for 30–45 seconds. Reconstituted baby milk may also be reheated in the microwave.

BACON

The microwave is an excellent method for cooking bacon with less shrinkage, no splattering and better shape retention than when conventionally cooked. Place a sheet of kitchen paper on a plate or dish and arrange layers of bacon rashers, overlapping fat and lean meat. Cover with another sheet of kitchen paper to avoid the fat spitting during cooking. Microwave on 100% High for 30–60 seconds per rasher, rotating the dish halfway through cooking time if several rashers are being cooked. Leave to stand for 2 minutes for evenly cooked, crisp rashers.

Thick slices and smoked rashers will take slightly longer to cook than thin or unsmoked rashers.

Bacon may also be cooked on a browning dish or roasting rack, following the manufacturer's instructions.

BANANAS

BAKED

Peel and split two large bananas lengthways, then cut in half (eight pieces). Place a single layer in a round dish and sprinkle with 4 tbsp orange and lemon juice and 1 tbsp brown sugar. Microwave on 100% High for 3 minutes. Serve hot with cream. Substitute 1 tbsp rum for 1 tbsp juice for a more exciting flavour.

BEETROOT

The microwave is an excellent timesaver when cooking this root crop. Place 450 g (1 lb) washed, even-sized beetroot in a bowl with 4 tbsp water. Microwave on 100% High for 5–7 minutes, tossing twice during cooking. Cool, then remove the skins with finger and thumb.

BEVERAGES

Heat one cup or mug of tea, coffee, chocolate, milk, etc. on 100% High for 1½–2 minutes.

BISCUITS

BASES

Bases for cheesecakes are easily made using the microwave. Melt 75 g (3 oz) unsalted butter and add one of the following crushed biscuits: 175 g (6 oz) plain digestives, chocolate digestives, ginger or rich tea biscuits. Mix well and press into a 18 cm (7 inch) dish. Useful as a topping for fruit fools and mousses.

See *Butter, melting*

RE-CRISPING

To re-crisp crackers and biscuits without fillings (e.g. not custard creams), place a sheet of kitchen paper on the base of the cooker and arrange a layer in a circle. Microwave on 100% High for a few seconds. Cool and store in an airtight container.

BLACKBERRIES

See *Fruit*

BOTTLING

FRUIT

Method and timing for one 500 ml (18 fl oz) jar. Microwave jars of fruit individually.

Pack the prepared fruit into a warmed sterilized jar and pour in the hot syrup. Cover with clingfilm. Microwave on 100% High for 2–3 minutes, then on (Low) Defrost for 3–4 minutes.

Use oven gloves to remove from the cooker. Cover, seal and label. The fruit will keep for up to two months.

See *Sterilizing*

BREAD

BAKING

When bread making, warm flour for 15 seconds on 100% High to assist in proving and rising dough.

Place dough in a lightly floured bowl. Cover and microwave on Low (Defrost) for 15 seconds. Stand for 10 minutes. Repeat until dough has doubled in size.

Microwaved bread doughs dry out much quicker than when conventionally cooked. To help prevent this, when cool wrap in a sealed polythene bag or plastic container.

As microwaved dough does not brown, sprinkle with sesame seeds, poppy seeds, bran, oats, or crushed grains before cooking. Recipes that use brown flours, sugar or eggs in the ingredients will look more appealing when cooked.

DEFROSTING

Cut loaves   May be left in the wrapping but remove any metal clip or seal. Microwave on Low (Defrost) for 5 minutes. If only a few slices are required, wrap in kitchen paper and microwave on 100% High for 8–12 seconds.

Uncut loaves   Wrap in kitchen paper to absorb the moisture and microwave on 100% High for 1½–2 minutes. A hard lump will remain in the centre, so stand for 5 minutes to finish the defrosting process. Bread will toughen if allowed to overheat.

Rolls, buns, scones, etc.   Do not microwave in plastic bags. Wrap in kitchen paper and microwave on Low (Defrost) for approximately 8 seconds each. For several rolls, place them in a ring on a sheet of kitchen paper and cover with another piece. Microwave as above, adjusting the time accordingly.

Teabreads   Can also be defrosted using this process. Reduce the time slightly according to the size of the loaf.

REFRESHING

Cut bread into slices and wrap in kitchen paper. Microwave on 100% High for 5–10 seconds for six slices.

FRENCH BREAD

Cheese   Cut the loaf into thick slices to within 1 cm (½ inch) of the base so leaving the loaf intact. Place alternate slices of processed Cheddar and Emmenthal cheese between the incisions. Place on a piece of kitchen paper and microwave on 50% Medium for 1–1½ minutes until the cheese has started to melt.

Serve with quiche, soups and salads.

Garlic   Cut loaf as above. Cream 125 g (4 oz) butter with 4 crushed garlic cloves and 1 tsp chopped parsley. Spread between the slices, wrap loosely in kitchen paper and microwave on 100% High for 1–1½ minutes.

Serve with soups and lasagne.

Herb   Substitute 1 tbsp fresh or dried herbs for garlic cloves.

FRENCH TOAST

Beat two eggs, 25 g (1 oz) melted butter and 2 tbsp milk together. Cut bread or French stick into 2.5 cm (1 inch) slices and dip in the egg mixture. Prepare a browning dish and microwave the toast on 100% High for ½–1 minute. Turn over and cook for a further ½–1 minute until browned.

If making sweet toast, add 1 tsp icing sugar and a pinch of nutmeg or cinnamon to the egg mixture.

If making savoury toast, add a pinch of salt and pepper to the mixture. Serve with breakfast foods or as a snack.

FRIED BREAD

Remove the crusts of two slices of brown or white bread. Butter on both sides, place on a shallow dish and microwave on 100% High for 40–60 seconds. Turn over and cook for 40–60 seconds. Top with scrambled or poached egg or tomatoes. A better result will be achieved if a browning dish is used.

PITTA BREAD

Warm pitta bread in the microwave to serve with soups, pâtés or dips. Wrap in kitchen paper and microwave on 100% High for a few seconds. As a tasty snack, split and fill the breads with ham, cheese, tomatoes, or chopped crisp salad vegetables. Place on a double layer of kitchen paper and microwave on 100% High for 45–60 seconds.

TOASTED SANDWICHES

Using the egg mixture for French toast (above), make up sweet or savoury sandwiches and dip in the batter. Prepare a browning dish and microwave one sandwich on 100% High for 1 minute. Turn over and cook for 1 minute more.

Alternatively, butter two slices of fresh crusty bread and make a sandwich with the filling between the unbuttered sides. Prepare a browning dish and microwave each side of the sandwich on 100% High for 30–45 seconds.

Serve as a tasty, quick snack.

See *Croissants*

BREADCRUMBS

Lay slices of brown or white bread on an upturned cardboard egg box for support and to assist the drying process evenly. Microwave on 100% High for 1–1½ minutes per slice. Leave until cold and the slices will crumb easily. Stale bread absorbs cooking juices much more than fresh.

BROWNING

Breadcrumbs are easily browned in the microwave to be used as a topping for casseroles and desserts or as a coating for fish, poultry and chops. Crumb 50 g (2 oz) brown or white bread including crusts in a processor or blender. Spread on kitchen paper and microwave on 100% High for 5–7 minutes until completely dry, tossing two or three times during cooking. Cool and store in an airtight container for up to six weeks.

FLAVOURING

To flavour browned or toasted breadcrumbs, add 1–2 tbsp parsley, thyme, chilli or curry powder, garlic salt, celery salt, microwave seasonings, dried citrus zest etc. Crushed wheat crackers, crushed cream crackers, oats, wheatflakes, sesame seeds, poppy seeds or coconut can be mixed with breadcrumbs for variety and used for a coating.

Use to coat skinned chicken joints, bacon steaks, escalopes, pork and lamb chops, or as a garnish and decoration for vegetables and desserts.

TOASTING

Place 25 g (1 oz) unsalted butter or margarine in a bowl and melt on 100% High for 1 minute. Add 125 g (4 oz) seasoned white breadcrumbs and mix together well. Spread half the mixture on a 20 cm (8 inch) plate and cook uncovered for 1 minute on 100% High. Stir to bring the outside browning crumbs into the centre and microwave on 100% High for 1 minute more. Repeat this process for the remaining breadcrumbs.

BROCCOLI

Try to choose heads and stalks of a uniform size. Trim the ends
from 225 g (8 oz) broccoli and arrange in a shallow dish with the
heads pointing towards the centre. Sprinkle with 4 tbsp water
and cover with pierced clingfilm. Microwave on 100% High for
6–8 minutes, giving the dish a half turn once during cooking
time. Leave to stand for 2 minutes. Drain and serve with lemon
butter, and a sprinkling of toasted almonds or sesame seeds.

See *Butter*, *Flavoured*

BROWNING AGENTS

There are a variety of browning agents that can be used to
improve the appearance of meats during cooking.

Brush with soy sauce, Worcestershire sauce combined with
water and melted butter, gravy browning, honey, paprika,
microwave seasoning, brown onion soup mix (reconstituted),
honey, brown and fruity sauces, barbecue sauce etc.

Whenever possible use unsalted butter as salt can toughen
food fibres, especially when cooking meat.

For recipes, see *Butter*, *Flavoured* and *Meat Glazes and Bastes*.

BROWNING DISHES

See *Dishes*

BRUSSELS SPROUTS

Cooking sprouts in the microwave gives particularly good results. They retain their crispness and colour and odours are cut to a minimum.

Wash and remove the outer leaves of 450 g (1 lb) sprouts and cut a small cross at the base. Place in a bowl with 4 tbsp water, cover and microwave for 6–7 minutes, tossing once during cooking.

Stand for 2–3 minutes, drain, season and serve with a sauce or lemon butter.

See *Butter*, *Flavoured* and *Sauces*

BUTTER

Whenever possible use unsalted butter in a baste as salt will toughen the food, especially when cooking meat.

BROWNING

Place 125 g (4 oz) butter in a heatproof dish. Cover and microwave on 100% High for 5–6 minutes, stirring three times during cooking. Skim off any foam and use to glaze vegetables to enhance their colour and appearance.

CLARIFYING

To clarify salted butter place 50 g (2 oz) in a bowl and cover with greaseproof paper to prevent spitting. Microwave on 100% High for 1 minute. The sediment can then be removed.
See *Fat*

FLAVOURED

Anchovy Melt 50 g (2 oz) unsalted butter, add 25 g (1 oz) drained and mashed anchovy fillets, 1 tbsp chopped parsley, black pepper and squeeze of lemon juice. Use as a glaze for fish.

Cheese   Melt 50 g (2 oz) unsalted butter. Add 1 tsp Parmesan cheese and seasoning.

Use as a glaze for whole sweetcorn. Sprinkle with parsley.

Garlic   Melt 50 g (2 oz) unsalted butter. Add a few shakes of garlic powder or 2 crushed fresh garlic cloves and seasoning.

Use as a glaze for grilled steaks, chops, potatoes and courgettes.

Herb   Melt 50 g (2 oz) unsalted butter. Add either 1 tsp parsley, mint, chives, thyme, etc. and seasoning.

Use as a glaze for potatoes, carrots, cauliflower, parsnips and poached fish.

Lemon or Orange   Melt 50 g (2 oz) unsalted butter and add 1 tbsp lemon or orange juice and seasoning.

Use as a glaze for asparagus, broccoli, carrots or poached fish. Garnish with the grated zest.

Liqueur   Soften 125 g (4 oz) unsalted butter and beat in 50 g (2 oz) sieved icing sugar and 2 tbsp brandy, rum or liqueur of your choice.

Use as a topping for Christmas pudding, rum babas, croissants, fruit flans or sponges.

A pat of savoury butter placed on cooked food improves its appearance and adds more flavour. Use the recipes above, but just soften the butter slightly instead of melting it. Place on a sheet of greaseproof paper and form into a roll. Chill in a refrigerator until hardened, then slice to garnish hot food.

See *Low Fat Spread*

MELTING

Place 25 g (1 oz) butter in a dish, cover and microwave on 100% High for 15–30 seconds.

SOFTENING

Remove the wrapper from 225 g (8 oz) butter and place in a dish. Microwave on Low (Defrost) for 1–1½ minutes and leave to stand for 2 minutes before use.

C

CABBAGE

Red, green, white, Savoy cabbage and Chinese leaves can be cooked using this method. Shred a combination of them to give a more interesting colour.

When cutting red cabbage use a stainless steel knife to stop it 'bleeding' and add 1 tsp vinegar to preserve its colour when cooking.

Serve cabbage with a basic white sauce topped with grated cheese, breadcrumbs, crisps or parsley to improve the appearance.

COOKING

Wash 450 g (1 lb) shredded cabbage and drain well. Place in a pierced boilable or roasting bag with a knob of butter. Microwave on 100% High for 6–8 minutes, tossing once during cooking. Salt, toss again and leave to stand for 2 minutes. Cabbage may also be cooked in a covered dish using the same method.

REMOVING LEAVES

The outer leaves of a cabbage are easily removed by microwaving for recipes requiring whole leaves, e.g. stuffed cabbage leaves. Simply wash the whole cabbage, place in a dish, cover and microwave on 100% High for 2–3 minutes. Approximately six outer leaves can then be removed. Repeat until required number have been loosened and blanched.

To make cabbage leaf parcels, trim away the hard centre at the base of each leaf, fill with stuffing and roll into neat parcels. Place eight in a dish with the seams underneath and cover with tomato sauce. Cover and microwave on 100% High for 8–10 minutes, turning the dish once and basting the parcel halfway through the cooking time. Stand for 3 minutes before serving. If a raw meat stuffing is used increase the cooking time accordingly.

See *Sauces* and *Stuffings*

CAKES

BASIC RULES

Do not grease and flour dishes as this will result in a hard crust forming on the outside of the cake. Instead line the dish with greaseproof paper or clingfilm or *very* lightly grease the dish but *do not* flour.

When cooking cakes, stand the dish on an upturned plate or saucer to encourage an even distribution of the microwaves.

Add custard powder to cakes or puddings to improve colour. Substitute 15 g (½ oz) custard powder for 15 g (½ oz) flour.

A cake will not spoil when the microwave door is opened, unlike conventional cooking. This means the dish can be turned frequently to ensure an even cooking of the mixture.

Microwaved sponges have a tendency to dry out. To prevent this, fill and ice when cool, wrap in foil or store in an airtight container. A stale uniced cake can be refreshed by microwaving on Low (Defrost) for 30 seconds.

Cocoa brings out the fat content in a cake mixture, making it heavy. For this reason use only 15 g (½ oz) cocoa to every 125 g (4 oz) fat.

CREAMED MIXTURES

Creamed mixtures will be lighter and have a better flavour if the butter and sugar are warmed for a few seconds before creaming.

FAIRY CAKES

To ensure that fairy cakes keep their shape during cooking if you do not have a microwave bun tray, use two cake cases or cut yoghurt pots so that cases fit inside them.

FILLINGS AND TOPPINGS

For quick and easy sponge cake fillings, use proprietary jars of spreads, e.g. hazelnut, chocolate, vanilla etc. Alternatively, use a can of pie filling to sandwich and top a sponge or fill a flan. To make a hot sauce for puddings and ice-cream, empty a can or jar of pie filling into a bowl, cover and microwave on 100% High for 2 minutes. Stir halfway through cooking time.

Another quick topping for sponges and ice-cream is a Mars Bar or some after dinner mints melted on 50% Medium for 1–2 minutes.

Decorate iced cakes with chopped nuts, flaked almonds, chocolate vermicelli, grated white, milk or plain chocolate, sieved icing sugar, cherries, glacé fruits and angelica, toasted coconut or citrus zest.

See *Icing*

Butter Cream Place 125 g (4 oz) unsalted butter, 350 g (12 oz) sieved icing sugar and 2 tbsp milk in a bowl. Microwave on 100% High for 1 minute. Add the grated rind and juice of one orange or lemon and beat until smooth. Use to ice and fill sponge cakes. This icing may also be flavoured with liquid coffee or essences, e.g. vanilla, almond, rum, pistachio etc. Omit the juice before flavouring.

Chocolate Place 125 g (4 oz) unsalted butter, 4 tbsp drinking chocolate powder, 300 g (10 oz) sieved icing sugar and 2 tbsp milk in a bowl. Microwave on 100% High for 3 minutes. Beat until thick and smooth. Cool. Use to fill and ice sponges and fairy cakes.

Toffee Place 125 g (4 oz) unsalted butter, 125 g (4 oz) soft brown sugar and 1 small can of condensed milk in a bowl. Microwave uncovered on 100% High for 4 minutes, stirring once halfway through the cooking time. Remove with oven gloves and beat until smooth. Leave to cool if using to sandwich and ice cakes, or serve hot with puddings and ice-cream.

This sauce can also be poured over shortbread and when cold spread with a layer of melted chocolate to make a caramel bar.

See *Shortbread*

FRUIT CAKES

Cook fruit cakes on Low (Defrost) to develop the flavour of the ingredients. Use dark brown sugar and 1 tsp gravy browning to ensure a rich colour.

If your fruit cake recipe does not cook through to the centre, use the following tips:

1. Use small eggs and reduce the liquid content slightly.
2. Make a well in the centre before cooking.
3. Wrap the cake in foil during the standing time.

SPONGE MIXTURES

Microwaved sponge mixtures need to be slightly wetter than conventional recipes. Add an extra 2 tbsp milk or water for a lighter and moister result.

As sponges do not brown on the surface when cooked in the microwave, improve their appearance by using brown sugar, a mixture of white and brown flour, treacle, chocolate or cocoa if possible. This will not be necessary if the sponge is to be iced or decorated after cooking.

CARROTS

New baby carrots cook much better than old as they are smaller and do not have a woody core.

NEW

To cook whole, wash, top and tail 350 g (12 oz) new carrots. Place in a dish with 2 tbsp water. Cover with pierced clingfilm and microwave on 100% High for 6–8 minutes, tossing once during cooking. Stand for 3 minutes. Drain, season and serve with orange butter or white sauce.

OLD

Peel, top and tail 225 g (8 oz) old carrots and cut into 5 mm (¼ inch) slices or wedges. Microwave for 4–7 minutes. Continue as for new.

See *Butter*, *Flavoured* and *Sauces*

CASSEROLES

Cheap, tough cuts of meat are not cooked successfully in the microwave as they need very long, slow cooking to break down the fibres. When cooking casseroles choose a more tender cut than when conventionally cooking or tenderize the meat in a marinade overnight. Microwave casseroles on 100% High until the liquid is boiling, then cook on 50% Medium or less if possible.

When microwaving casseroles or stews, grease will rise to the surface. Remove with a spoon or kitchen paper during cooking.

To give a good result, cut the ingredients into even-sized pieces and stir the casserole frequently to ensure an even distribution of heat. Turn the dish regularly to assist in even cooking.

See *Marinades*

CAULIFLOWER

To cook a 450 g (1 lb) cauliflower whole, trim the outside leaves away and cut the stalk off as close as possible to the florets. Wash well but do not dry and wrap in wet greaseproof paper.

Place in a dish, stalk uppermost and microwave on 100% High for 4–5 minutes. Turn the whole cauliflower over and microwave for a further 4–5 minutes. Leave to stand for 2 minutes. Season and coat with melted butter, parsley or cheese sauce. Sprinkle with a crisp garnish.

See *Sauces* and *Garnishes*

CELERY

Microwaved celery retains its crunchy texture and golden colour.

HEARTS

Slice celery hearts in half and for each heart add 2 tbsp water. Place a single layer in a dish, cover and microwave on 100% High. Four hearts will take 5–6 minutes. Stock can be used instead of water to give a fuller flavour. Serve as below.

SLICED

Separate stalks, trim ends and wash in cold water. Slice into 1 cm (½ inch) pieces and place in a dish with 2 tbsp water and 25 g (1 oz) butter. Cover and microwave on 100% High for 4–5 minutes, tossing once during cooking. Stand for 2 minutes.

Drain and serve with a flavoured white sauce or on their own with a glaze of melted butter and black pepper.

See *Sauces* and *Butter, Flavoured*

CEREALS

To re-crisp soft cereals, spread one or two servings on a large plate lined with kitchen paper and place in the microwave with a cup of water. Depending on the staleness of the cereals, microwave on 100% High for 30 seconds to 3 minutes, tossing every 30 seconds and testing for crispness.

CHAPATIS

Reheat chapatis in the microwave. Place two on a plate and microwave on 100% High for approximately 1 minute until swollen and hot.

CHEESE

CHEESE ON TOAST

Cheese becomes softer when microwaved than grilled, but if overcooked in the microwave it will become tough and stringy. For a good result take one slice of buttered toast and top with grated or sliced cheese. Place on a sheet of kitchen paper in the centre of the cooker and microwave for 10–30 seconds.

CREAM CHEESE

Cream cheese and cheese spreads will spread easily if microwaved on Low (Defrost) for a few seconds. Remove any foil covering before microwaving.

REHEATING CHEESE DISHES

Do not reheat cheese recipes from frozen. Allow the meal to thaw first otherwise the cheese will cook before the other ingredients and could be stringy and tough. Only add cheese as a topping during the last couple of minutes of microwaving whenever possible.

RIPENING

Soft cheese can be ripened in the microwave, e.g. Camembert, Brie, Stilton.

Place 225 g (8 oz) cheese on a serving board (not wooden) and microwave on Low (Defrost) for 15–45 seconds depending on the condition of the cheese. Leave to stand for 5 minutes before serving. Harder cheeses may be brought to room temperature by using the method above and microwaved for slightly longer.

CHEESECAKES

See *Biscuits, Bases*

CHESTNUTS

SKINNING AND COOKING

Chestnuts can be skinned and cooked using the microwave. Take 225 g (8 oz) chestnuts and make a slit in their skins using a sharp knife. Place in a heatproof bowl and pour over 600 ml (1 pt) boiling water. Microwave on 100% High for 7–10 minutes, drain and cool slightly. The outer casing and skin can then be removed easily.

CREAMED

Soak 125 g (4 oz) dried chestnuts overnight. Drain and place in a bowl with 150 ml (¼ pt) boiling water. Cover with a lid and microwave on 100% High for 5 minutes, stirring once during cooking. Cool with the remaining juices and cream in a liquidizer or food processor. Use for stuffings and cake fillings.

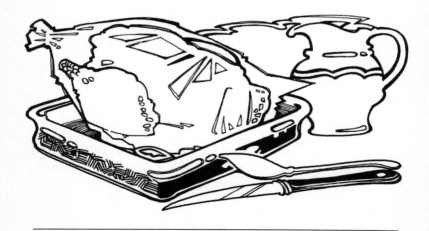

CHICKEN

Chicken cooks beautifully in the microwave, because the meat remains moist and flavoursome. However, the skin will not crisp and turn golden brown: to improve the appearance, brush the bird with a browning agent before cooking or serve coated with a sauce. Cook the chicken on an upturned saucer placed in a dish or on a roasting rack to allow the juices to run away.

Place the bird in a roasting bag, or cover with greaseproof paper to assist browning. If using a roasting bag, cut the corner off so that the juices can drain away during cooking.

Microwave breast side down for one third of the cooking time, drain the juices, turn over and continue cooking. Wrap in foil shiny side inwards, stand for 5–8 minutes. To test if the bird is cooked there should be no trace of pink when the flesh is pierced between the leg joint and breast. Use the drained juices to make a gravy or sauce.

Microwave chicken on 100% High for 6 minutes per 450 g (lb) or 50% Medium for 9 minutes per 450 g (lb).

BONED AND STUFFED

Follow the same basic rules as cooking chicken. Do not pack stuffing too tightly. Weigh the stuffed bird and calculate the cooking time for 9–10 minutes per 450 g (lb). Microwave on 100% High for the first 6 minutes then on 50% Medium for the remainder of the timing. Turn the dish frequently and drain away the juices during cooking. (A stuffed whole chicken is best microwaved on 50% Medium setting.)

BRAISED

Microwave on 100% High for 8–9 minutes per 450 g (lb).

DRUMSTICKS

Cook drumsticks unseasoned or choose a coating of breadcrumbs, stuffing mix, etc. Place eight drumsticks in a circle on a plate, prepared browning dish or roasting rack with the thinner part of the drumstick towards the centre. Microwave on 100% High for 12–14 minutes, turning over halfway through cooking.

Stand for 2–3 minutes, serve hot or cold with a sauce or relish.

See *Browning Agents, Coatings, Sauces, Meat Glazes and Bastes*

CHIPS

See *Potatoes*

CHOCOLATE

MELTING

Place 125 g (4 oz) chocolate in a bowl and microwave on 50% Medium or Low (Defrost) for 2 minutes. Stir halfway through cooking time and allow to stand for 1 minute before using. If smaller amounts than this are melted, place half a cup of water in the cooker with the chocolate to prevent possible sparking.

CHUTNEY

Chutneys can be made successfully in the microwave. The advantages are that odours are cut to a minimum, there is no condensation and they cook quickly. Follow the basic rules of making jam for safety and to ensure a good finished result.

See *Jam*

CITRUS

FRUITS

Heat oranges, lemons, limes or grapefruits in the microwave on 100% High for 30 seconds each. You will be able to extract almost twice as much juice and the fruit will be easier to squeeze.

ZEST

This is a useful ingredient to flavour sweet and savoury dishes. To dry zest in the microwave, finely grate the rind from one medium or two small oranges, lemons or limes. Spread evenly on a plate and place in the microwave with a cup of water. Cook on 100% High for 4–6 minutes until zest is dry to the touch. Check at 1 minute intervals while cooking, rubbing between fingers and thumb to separate the particles. Leave to stand until dry (at least 3 hours) and store in an airtight jar for up to two months. When using dried zest in a recipe, only half the amount is needed as for fresh.

CLINGFILM

See *Covering Food* and page 9.

COATINGS

Meat that does not brown naturally in the microwave can be sprinkled and dipped in a crunchy coating to add 'bite', extra flavour and colour. Coatings also help to keep meat moist. Brush chops, steaks, drumsticks, etc. with beaten egg, then dip into coating mixture pressing it on well. Some meats may need to be dipped in egg and coated twice to ensure that the flesh is covered. Microwave on a browning dish or rack for the usual time, turning at intervals to ensure even cooking.

If the meat is microwaved on a plate or dish do not turn over during cooking. The surface will then keep crisp.

For speed, use stuffing mixes or convenience packets of coatings. Dried breadcrumbs can also be used.

See *Breadcrumbs*

COCOA

Cocoa has a tendency to bring out the fat content in a cake mixture, making it heavy. For this reason use only 15 g (½ oz) to each 125 g (4 oz) fat.

COCONUT

To toast coconut place 25 g (1 oz) in a dish and microwave on 100% High for 1 minute, tossing several times during cooking until golden brown.

COFFEE

BEANS, REFRESHING

Coffee beans can be refreshed in the microwave to restore their aroma and taste. Put 2 tbsp in a bowl lined with kitchen paper and place in the cooker with a cup of water. Microwave on 100% High for 30 seconds, tossing halfway through cooking time. Cool, grind and use as freshly roasted beans.

MAKING PERCOLATED COFFEE

Fresh, roasted beans are best for a full flavour. Put 2 tbsp ground coffee in a heatproof jug and pour over 600 ml (1 pt) cold water, stirring well. Microwave on 100% High for 4–5 minutes until very hot but not boiling. Cover and leave to infuse for 4–5 minutes for the flavour to develop. Strain, reheat for 1 minute and serve.

REHEATING

Make a full pot of coffee in a percolator or coffee machine. Reheat a cold cup or mug of coffee as required on 100% High for 1½–2 minutes. The coffee will taste as good as freshly made.

COURGETTES

Because of their high water content, courgettes cook beautifully in the microwave without the addition of liquid. They also retain their crispness and bright colour. Wash, top and tail 450 g (1 lb) courgettes. Cut into even-sized slices and place in a dish with 25 g (1 oz) butter. Cover and microwave on 100% High for 4–6 minutes, tossing once during cooking. Season and stand for 2 minutes. Drain and serve with flavoured butter or cheese sauce.

See *Butter, Flavoured* and *Sauces*

COVERING FOOD

Covering food during microwaving prevents spattering, holds in moisture, keeping it tender and soft, and assists in shortening the cooking time. Because moisture is retained, less, little or no liquid is required during microwaving, unlike conventional cookery.

When a tight-fitting cover is required in a recipe place a sheet of greaseproof paper underneath a casserole lid.

Use a tight covering of clingfilm when cooking foods that need little or no added liquid. Pierce or roll back clingfilm at one edge when cooking foods with a high liquid content or those which produce a lot of steam. Failure to do this may cause the clingfilm to explode as the steam cannot escape. (Unless using microwave clingfilm, such as Purecling and Saran Wrap, do not let ordinary clingfilm touch food.)

Kitchen paper stops splattering, absorbs moisture and allows steam to escape. Use to cover fatty food, e.g. when cooking bacon etc. and for heating breads, etc. when the moisture of the food needs to be absorbed to keep it crisp.

Greaseproof paper also prevents splattering and is used when moisture need not be retained in the food.

Roasting bags are ideal for cooking food in the microwave. They assist in browning food and are particularly useful when cooking joints of meat and poultry. Moisture is kept inside the bag, making the food more succulent, and because no spitting can occur the inside of the cooker is kept clean. Tie the bags loosely with string or use an elastic band. When cooking meats, snip off one corner of the bag so that the juices can drain away.

CREAM

DAIRY WHIPPED

To thaw 250 ml (9 fl oz) frozen cream, remove foil lid and cover with clingfilm. Microwave on Low (Defrost) for 2½–3 minutes. Stand for 5 minutes, stir lightly and serve.

DOUBLE

Place 600 ml (1 pt) double cream pieces, portions or flakes in a bowl and microwave on Low (Defrost) for 5 minutes, turning over halfway through cooking time. Stir and stand for 5 minutes before serving.

CROISSANTS

To warm croissants, place two on a sheet of kitchen paper inside the cooker with a small glass of water. Microwave on 100% High for 30–45 seconds. The water helps to keep the croissant moist. Serve immediately with butter, jam or melted chocolate. Alternatively, split and butter a cold croissant and fill with ham, cheese, tomato or filling of your choice. Place on a sheet of kitchen paper inside the cooker and microwave on 100% High for 45–60 seconds until the filling is hot. This makes a quick tasty snack.

CROUTONS

Remove crusts from 175 g (6 oz) white, brown or wholemeal bread and dice into 1 cm (½ inch) cubes. Spread a single layer in a dish and microwave on 100% High for 3–4 minutes, tossing every minute until dry. For flavouring, toss the bread cubes with one of the following and microwave as above.

Garlic Melt 25 g (1 oz) butter with two cloves of crushed garlic or 1 tsp garlic salt.

Herb Melt 25 g (1 oz) butter, add 2 tsp mixed herbs, pinch of salt and pepper.

Parsley Melt 25 g (1 oz) butter, add 2 tsp chopped parsley, pinch of salt and pepper.

Savoury Melt 25 g (1 oz) butter, add 1 tsp chicken seasoning.

CRUMBLES

As crumbles do not brown in the microwave, use wholemeal flour and demerara sugar instead of white. Add chopped nuts for a crisp, crunchy texture.

Often the fruit juice in crumbles and puddings bubbles over during cooking. To prevent this from happening, stir in 1 tsp cornflour to every 225 g (8 oz) fruit before microwaving.

CURDS

Orange, lemon, grapefruit or lime curds are easily made in the microwave using either a conventional or microwave recipe.

To set 450 g (1 lb) of curd, place rind, juice, sugar and butter in a bowl and microwave on 100% High for 2 minutes. Stir and add the beaten eggs. Microwave on 100% High for a further 3–4 minutes, stirring well at 30-second intervals. Do not let the mixture boil as it could curdle. If necessary, reduce the power setting. When thickened, pour into warmed, sterilized jars and store in the refrigerator for two to four weeks.

See *Sterilizing*

CUSTARD

Make perfect custard every time in the microwave. Whisk together 2 tbsp custard powder, 2 tbsp sugar and 600 ml (1 pt) milk in a large jug. Microwave on 100% High for 2 minutes. Whisk well, microwave for a further 3–4 minutes on 50% Medium, whisking twice during cooking.

Increase the custard powder by 1 tbsp if a thicker custard is required to flavour and set in a mould or for a trifle.

CONFECTIONERS'–Crème Pâtissière

Confectioners' custard is a beautiful creamy filling used to sandwich puff pastries, choux pastries, sponges and as a base for fruit flans. It may also be used as a base for fruit fools. Quick and simple to make in the microwave.

Recipe 1   Blend 150 ml (¼ pt) milk with 1 tbsp castor sugar and 1 tbsp cornflour. Microwave on 100% High for 1½–2 minutes, stirring once during cooking. Add 1 egg yolk and a few drops of vanilla essence and beat well. Microwave on 100% High for 1–2 minutes until thick and creamy, whisking every 30 seconds. Do not allow it to boil. Remove from the cooker, cover to prevent a skin forming and leave to cool. Chill well before using to fill cakes and pastries. Add 15 g (½ oz) butter to the custard for a creamier filling.

Recipe 2   Blend 25 g (1 oz) flour, 25 g (1 oz) castor sugar with 1 egg. Microwave 150 ml (¼ pt) milk on 100% High for 1½–2 minutes. Pour over blended ingredients and whisk well. Microwave on 50% Medium for 1½–2 minutes until thick and creamy, whisking every 30 seconds. Do not allow it to boil. Flavour with a little vanilla essence. Cover, cool and use as above.

POURING EGG CUSTARD

Using a microwave for this recipe saves the bother of using double saucepans, and the custard is less likely to curdle.

Place 300 ml (½ pt) milk, 2 egg yolks and 25 g (1 oz) caster sugar in a bowl and whisk together. Microwave on 100% High for 3–4 minutes, whisking four times during cooking. Do not allow the custard to boil otherwise the eggs will curdle. If necessary, reduce the power setting. When cooked, the mixture should be thick enough to coat the back of a wooden spoon. Flavour with a few drops of vanilla essence.

D

DEFROSTING

When defrosting meat, unwrap then microwave on Low (Defrost). As a guide, 450 g (1lb) will take 5–10 minutes. Never completely defrost meat, poultry or fish in the microwave as the outside of the food will begin to dry out around the edges and may even start to cook. Remove when still cool and icy in the centre and leave to stand at room temperature to finish thawing.

When defrosting foods which have a high liquid content, e.g. sauces, soups, casseroles, etc., stir them as soon as possible, bringing the thawed edges into the centre and breaking into lumps when soft enough. If your microwave does not have a Low or Defrost control, heat on 100% High for 30 seconds then stand for at least 2 minutes. Repeat this process until the food is thawed, turning and repositioning the food each time it is heated.

As the variety of puddings, desserts and cakes is endless, it is difficult to advise on a power setting and timing. Refer to the manufacturer's instructions and if in doubt thaw them on Low or Defrost.

As a guide cover most foods with clingfilm, kitchen paper or place in a covered dish when thawing in a microwave.

DISHES

ARE THEY SAFE?

If in doubt as to whether a dish is microwave safe, put it in the cooker with a cup containing 150 ml (¼ pt) water. Microwave on 100% High for 1–2 minutes. If the dish remains cool to touch when the water is hot it is safe to use for microwave cooking.

BROWNING

It is important to follow the manufacturer's instructions when using a browning dish.

Browning dishes are versatile and produce a similar effect to grilling and frying. When food is placed on a hot browning dish, press it down using a spatula to give a better contact and increase the browning process. Do not cut food in the dish as it could damage the surface. Use oven gloves to remove the dish from the cooker as the underneath becomes very hot. Place a hot browning dish on a heatproof surface.

Use heat-resistant plastic or wooden utensils to turn and stir food on a browning dish or casserole.

CLAY

Glazed or not these dishes are excellent for microwave cookery, especially when cooking less tender cuts of meat. Soak the lid and dish in cold water for 10 minutes before use.

SIZE AND SHAPE

Use roughly the same principle when choosing size as for conventional cooking. If the food is likely to boil over, e.g. when heating milk, making chutneys, preserves, sauces, etc. make sure that the container is only half full before boiling point is reached.

High-sided dishes will shield the food being cooked so lessening the risk of sudden burning.

Shallow dishes hasten cooking time as the microwaves can reach the food more easily.

When possible choose dishes of an even shape with rounded corners if circular dishes are not suitable.

Food will also cook more evenly if the dish is given a half turn during cooking.

Ring-shaped dishes cook foods well if they cannot be stirred or turned. The microwaves are able to cook the food from the centre as well as from the outside, giving a more even and quicker result.

Stand a glass open end up in the middle of a round dish to make a ring dish for bread and cake making.

STRAW BASKETS

Straw baskets are useful for warming rolls, bread, teacakes, etc. because of the short cooking time required. Also the food may be warmed and served in the same dish, e.g. for use at a dinner party.

WOOD

As wood contains small amounts of moisture which evaporate during microwaving, dishes, bowls or boards should not be used in the microwave as they could crack.

DOUGH

See *Bread*, *Pizzas*

DUCK

Wash the duck inside and out and dry well. Tie legs and wings to form a neat shape and prick the skin all over to help release the fatty juices during cooking. Place an upturned saucer in a large dish and lay the duck on this breast side down. The fat and juice can then drain away easily. Alternatively, cook duck on a roasting rack. Cover loosely with greaseproof paper or an opened roasting bag to prevent spitting.

Microwave the duck on 100% High for 7–9 minutes per 450 g (1 lb). After one-quarter of the cooking time, drain the juices away and turn breast uppermost. Brush with a baste, glaze or browning agent and continue cooking, turning the dish and basting twice. Remove from the microwave, wrap in foil (shiny side inwards) and rest for 15 minutes. To test if the duck is cooked, insert a skewer through the thickest part of the leg. The flesh should be slightly pink and the juices clear.

Skim the fat from the drained juices and use the juices to enrich the flavour of an accompanying sauce.

STUFFED

If stuffing the cavity of a duck, weigh the bird after doing so to calculate the cooking time correctly.

See *Browning agents, Meat Glazes and Bastes*

DUMPLINGS

Dumplings can be cooked on top of a casserole or on their own. Add grated cheese, herbs and spices to the suet dough to give a variety of flavours. For a better appearance and flavour, brush dumplings with water and coat with savoury stuffing mixes.

To cook, place dumplings in a circle on a sheet of grease-proof paper and microwave on 100% High. Six average-sized dumplings will take 4–5 minutes. Leave to stand for 1 minute before serving.

E

EGGS

When cooking eggs conventionally the white sets before the yolk, but when cooked in the microwave the reverse happens and the yolk cooks first. The reason for this occurrence is that the yolk contains more fat than the white therefore attracting more microwave energy. If the egg is cooked until the white is set the yolk will be very hard. Because of this the standing time after microwaving is very important.

BAKED

Break two eggs into ramekin dishes or on a heated browning dish and prick the yolks with a cocktail stick. Cover with pierced clingfilm and microwave on 50% Medium for 2 minutes, turning dishes once during cooking. Leave to stand for 1–2 minutes. If using a browning dish reduce the cooking time by 20–30 seconds.

OMELETTE

Omelettes are quick to make when cooked in the microwave but will not brown in the dish. If cooking a plain omelette, lightly grease a 20 cm (8 inch) shallow dish with butter. Pour in the beaten egg mixture and microwave on 50% Medium for 3–4 minutes, turning the dish twice during cooking. Add meat and vegetables before or during cooking for a savoury omelette (calculating their cooking time accordingly).

Sweet omelettes can be made as above. Spread with warmed jam or fill with fruit after cooking. Fold in half and sprinkle with icing sugar.

To make a puffy, light omelette, separate four eggs. Beat the yolks with 2 tbsp milk and a pinch of sugar or seasonings (for sweet or savoury). Whisk egg whites until stiff and fold into the yolk mixture. Microwave on 50% Medium for 5–7 minutes until the centre is set.

PIERCING

When microwaving a whole broken egg always pierce the yolk at least once with a cocktail stick to break the membrane. Failure to do this will result in the egg exploding during cooking.

SCRAMBLED

Break an egg into a buttered dish and beat with 1 tbsp of milk, a knob of butter and a little seasoning. Cover and microwave on High for 30 seconds, then stir well. Cover again and microwave for a further 10–15 seconds. Stir again, then leave to stand for 2 minutes and serve at once. Do not overcook the eggs otherwise they will become leathery.

POACHED

Place 2 tbsp water and ¼ tsp vinegar into a ramekin dish. Cover and microwave on 100% High for 30–40 seconds or until boiling. Break an egg into the dish and pierce yolk. Cover with pierced clingfilm and microwave on 50% Medium for 15–30 seconds. Stand for 1 minute before serving. For more than one egg turn the dishes halfway through cooking time and adjust the timing accordingly.

SCRAMBLED

Scrambled eggs cooked in the microwave are fluffier and have more volume than if conventionally cooked. Place 15 g (½ oz) butter in a bowl and microwave on 100% High for a few seconds until melted. Beat in two eggs and 2 tbsp milk. Microwave on 100% High for 2–2¼ minutes, stirring with a fork halfway through cooking time. Season, mix thoroughly, cover and leave to stand for 1½ minutes as the mixture will continue to cook.

Butter in the recipe may be omitted for the calorie conscious as it is only used for flavour. Also the milk may be replaced by water. The result is a less creamy mixture.

TEMPERATURE

To bring a refrigerated egg to room temperature, microwave on 100% High for 5 seconds. Do not microwave for longer as it may explode. If you do not have a digital timer on your microwave cooker, check the timing by using the second hand of a watch, timer or clock.

WHITE

An egg white at room temperature will whisk to a much greater volume than one that has been refrigerated.

YOLK

Refrigerated eggs are more likely to curdle when mixed with butter or oil. Bring them to room temperature by beating 2 yolks in a bowl and microwave on 100% High for 10 seconds. This should then prevent them from curdling.

F

FAT

Clarify fat after roasting or boiling meats by placing it in a bowl with a little water. Microwave on 100% High until it starts to boil, strain and leave to set. The sediment will fall to the bottom and the clarified fat can be removed from the top. Place this in a clean bowl, melt on Low (Defrost) and pour into a clean container. Cool, cover and keep in the refrigerator for up to four weeks.

FISH

Microwaved fish retains its delicate flavour and unlike meat does not need browning to appeal to the eye. The appearance of cooked fish can be transformed with the addition of garnishes, sauces and flavoured butters.

The microwave is an excellent method of cooking fish as all the moisture and odours are retained in the covered dish. Only microwave until the fish starts to flake, then stand for 2 minutes to ensure the centre or thicker part is thoroughly cooked.

Always score the skin on fish two or three times before cooking and remove the eyes if cooked whole, or they will burst.

CAKES AND FINGERS

These can be cooked in the microwave without being defrosted.

Melt a little butter or margarine and brush the fingers or cakes on both sides. Lay six on a prepared browning dish or buttered plate and microwave on 100% High for 3 minutes, rearranging two or three times during cooking and turning over once. (The use of a browning dish will produce better results.)

HERRINGS – Pickled (Rollmops)

Remove the heads and tails of four cleaned herrings. Fillet and roll up, skin side out, securing each one with a wooden cocktail stick. Place a single layer in a dish and sprinkle with 1 onion, finely sliced, 2 tsp sugar, 10 whole peppercorns, 4 bay leaves, 2 tsp pickling spice, 300 ml (½ pt) cider vinegar.

Cover and microwave for 8–10 minutes, rearranging herrings halfway through cooking time. Uncover and cool the herrings in the juices.

Chill in the refrigerator before serving as a starter or with salads.

KIPPERS

Frozen bagged kippers are easily microwaved, retaining most of their odours. To cook a small bag from frozen, pierce and put on a plate. Microwave on 100% High for 4 minutes and leave to stand for 2 minutes to finish cooking before serving.

POACHING

Poached fish is cooked in a small amount of liquid (e.g. lemon juice, water, milk, fish stock, white wine). Unlike meat this may be seasoned with salt and poured over the fish without any danger of toughening or drying it out.

Lay 450 g (1lb) fish fillets, cutlets or steaks in a dish, add liquid, cover and microwave on 100% High for 4–6 minutes. Thicker fleshed fish, e.g. cod, will take at least 6 minutes as will stuffed fillets. Whole fish will take 5–7 minutes. Stand for 2–3 minutes before serving.

ROE

Soft roe cooks beautifully in the microwave. As no liquid is needed to cook them, their true flavour can be appreciated. Prick 225 g (8 oz) of roes a few times to break the membrane and place a single layer in a buttered dish. Cover and microwave on 100% High for 2 minutes. Turn and rearrange the roes and cook for a further 2 minutes. Season with black pepper and stand for 2 minutes before serving. Roes are a lovely snack served on toast, topped with lemon sauce and sprinkled with chopped parsley.

TROUT

Clean and prepare the fish, season inside and arrange on a shallow dish, head to tail. Dot with butter and sprinkle over a little lemon juice. Cover with a lid and microwave on 100% High until the fish just begins to flake. Stand for 2–3 minutes before serving. Trout may be stuffed, if preferred. Weigh the fish and microwave for 4 minutes per 450 g (1 lb) in either case.

Serve with a sprinkling of toasted almonds or a small carton of soured cream mixed with 1 tsp chopped parsley. Warm for 45–60 seconds on 100% High. Pour over the trout and garnish with watercress and lemon slices.

WHOLE BREADED

Use the same method as for fish fingers. Two portions of breaded plaice will take 4–5 minutes from frozen, rearranging and turning over once during cooking.

See *Butter, Flavoured, Stocks* and *Sauces*

FLAMBÉEING

Warm brandy, etc. in the microwave when required for flambéed foods.

However, heating spirits of any kind in a microwave carries an element of risk if left unattended. The spirit should only be allowed to warm but not reach anywhere near boiling point otherwise it could ignite. About 2 tbsp spirit or liqueur will take no longer than 15–20 seconds on 100% High. For safety, measure the amount of spirit required and pour into a heat-proof container and warm. Do not use a wine glass.

FLOUR

When bread making, warm flour for 15 seconds on 100% High to assist in proving and rising dough.

FOIL

Most manufacturers state that small pieces of foil can be used in the microwave provided that certain safety measures are adhered to. Refer to your personal handbook for their specific instructions.

Foil is a good conductor of heat and is used mainly for keeping food hot and to complete its cooking during the standing time. Wrap food in foil with the shiny side in to reflect the heat back into the food.

FONDUE

Do not try to keep fondues constantly hot in the microwave as they can curdle with excessive prolonged heating. As soon as the ingredients are melted, blended and hot, pour into a fondue warmer and serve. Microwaved fondues tend to be a little thinner in consistency than when conventionally cooked, so thicken with a little cornflour or increase the quantity slightly in the recipe.

FRUIT

DRIED

Dried fruit may be swollen to full capacity in the microwave without soaking beforehand. Put 125 g (4 oz) dried fruit (e.g. raisins, mixed fruit, sultanas, etc.) in a shallow dish and sprinkle with 3 tbsp water. Cover with pierced clingfilm and microwave on 100% High for 3 minutes until soft. Stir two or three times during cooking. Leave to stand for 3 minutes, cool and drain before using.

Alcohol may be used instead of water: use 4 tbsp. Stir several times during cooking otherwise spot burning may occur because of the high concentration of sugar.

When cooking larger fruits (e.g. apricots, figs, pears, peaches) a better result will be obtained if they are soaked overnight in cold water, then drained and cooked as above.

EXTRACTING JUICE

See *Citrus, Fruits*

PEELING

Depending on the size of individual fruits, the timing given for peeling can vary considerably. Microwave larger fruit, such as peaches, for 15–20 seconds, microwave two smaller fruits, like apricots, for 15–20 seconds. Stand for 1 minute before removing the skin.

POACHING

Poach fruit whole with sugar syrup when serving as a dessert, to increase their succulence, taste and appearance. As a general guide to poaching fresh fruit, prick the skins if cooking whole so that they do not burst. Place 450 g (1 lb) in a dish with 300 ml (½ pt) sugar syrup, cover with pierced clingfilm and microwave on 100% High for 3–6 minutes. Stir once during cooking.

When poaching fruit to soften for use in flans, pies or for the calorie conscious, place in a bowl with 1 tbsp water, cover with pierced clingfilm and microwave on 100% High for 3–4 minutes. Stir once during cooking if the fruit is halved and stoned. Stand for 2–3 minutes before serving.

If wished, stone the fruit and reduce with 150 ml (¼ pt) of syrup to a purée in a liquidizer or food processor. Use as a sauce for ice-cream, sponge puddings, etc. or add to confectioners' custard to make a rich fruit fool.

Greengages and plums can be microwaved without using sugar syrup or additional water as they are very juicy. They hold their shape well and make a good filling for flan cases. Halve and stone 450 g (1 lb) fruit and arrange cut side down in a dish. Cover and microwave on 100% High for 2–3 minutes, rearranging and turning the dish once during cooking. Cool and use as required.

BERRY FRUITS

Prick the skins and microwave as above for 1–3 minutes if poaching, 3–5 minutes if puréeing. If puréeing, only use 2 tbsp sugar syrup otherwise it will be watery. Sweeten the purée with sugar if it is too tart.

GLACÉ FRUITS

Glacé fruits can be made by preparing a caramel syrup in the microwave. Choose fresh strawberries, orange segments, grapes, pineapple pieces OR tinned peaches, apricots, maraschino cherries, provided the fruit is drained and dried beforehand.

Lightly brush a dish or plate with oil. Place 125 g (4 oz) sugar and 5 tbsp hot water in a deep jug. Microwave uncovered on 100% High for 1½–2 minutes until the sugar has dissolved. Stir once during cooking. Add 1 tsp glucose powder, stir well and microwave on 100% High for 5–6 minutes until it just starts to turn brown. Check the syrup frequently for this.

Place the jug of syrup on a wet cloth to reduce the temperature or add 1 tsp water. As soon as it stops boiling, spear the fruits on cocktail sticks and dip in the syrup. Shake off excess syrup and leave to set on the prepared dish. When cool and crisp place in paper cases.

See *Sugar Syrup*

G

GAME

Game cooks best on a 50% Medium setting. Use a browning agent to coat the skin if a deeper colour is preferred or cook in a roasting bag. This will also keep the meat moist and assist in browning it.

As a guide, microwave game on 50% Medium for 8–10 minutes per 450 g (lb). Use the same setting and timing if casseroling.

Do not overcook game as the flesh becomes dry and very tough.

RABBIT

Follow the same basic rules as microwaving chicken. Rabbit cooks particularly well in a casserole.

See *Chicken*

GARNISHES

Microwave cookery is a moist form of heat, which softens ingredients, but does not brown them.

Try to use crisp garnishes whenever possible to give more 'bite' to a food and improve its appearance.

Sprinkle vegetables and sauces with: crushed crisps, browned breadcrumbs, nuts, crushed crackers and cornflakes, crisp fried bacon pieces, cheese, crushed dried onion rings.

GELATINE

To dissolve gelatine, place 3 tbsp water in a bowl and sprinkle over 1 level tbsp gelatine. Leave for a couple of minutes until firm then microwave on 100% High for 1 minute until gelatine is dissolved. Stir well before using.

GOOSEBERRIES

See *Fruit*

GLAZES

See *Butter, Flavoured* and *Meat Glazes and Bastes*

GRAPEFRUIT

To 'grill' a grapefruit in the microwave, halve, loosen the segments and place in a dish. Pour over 1 tbsp rum or sherry and sprinkle with 2 tsp brown sugar. Microwave on 100% High for 1 minute. Top with a maraschino cherry and serve as a quick starter.

See *Citrus, Curds*

GRAPES

FROSTING

Break a bunch of grapes into stems of two or three and dip into 1 egg white, lightly beaten, tapping off any excess liquid. Dip into castor sugar, coating generously and taking care not to sugar stalks. Place a piece of greaseproof paper on the base of the cooker and arrange the grapes in a circle. Microwave on Low (Defrost) for approximately 3 minutes, turning over halfway through cooking time. The sugar casing should be dry and crisp to the touch. Use frosted grapes to decorate special desserts, e.g. soufflés, flans, pavlovas.

GRAVY

To make a quick and simple gravy, place 2 tsp meat dripping, 1 tbsp plain flour and 300 ml (½ pt) meat juices/stock in a jug. Whisk well and microwave on 100% High for 2–3 minutes, whisking twice during cooking. Season with salt and pepper. Darken the gravy with a little browning if a richer colour is preferred.

GREENGAGES

See *Fruit, Poaching*

GREASEPROOF PAPER

See *Covering Food*

H

HAZELNUTS

To roast and skin hazelnuts, put 50 g (2 oz) shelled nuts in a dish and microwave on 100% High for 2–2½ minutes, tossing two or three times during cooking. Cool and rub nuts between hands to remove skins.

HERBS

DRYING

Wash and dry well. Spread a layer on a sheet of kitchen paper and place on the base of the cooker with a cup of water. Cover with another sheet of paper and microwave on 100% High until the herbs dull in colour and crumble easily. Rearrange several times during cooking and check for dryness at 30-second intervals. Leave to cool, crumble and store in an airtight jar in a cool dark place.

See *Seasonings*

HONEY

To melt honey which has crystallized, heat on 50% Medium or Low (Defrost) for 20–60 seconds, removing the metal lid before placing jar in the microwave.

I

ICE CREAM

MAKING

Ice-creams are easily made in the microwave using an egg custard base.

Place 300 ml (½ pt) milk and 125 g (4 oz) castor sugar in a bowl. Microwave on 100% High for 2–2½ minutes, stirring once during cooking. The milk should not boil, but be warm enough to dissolve the sugar. Whisk in 2 beaten eggs and 1 tsp vanilla essence and microwave on 100% High for 2–3 minutes, whisking twice during cooking. The custard should thicken and be smooth. Cool and fold in 300 ml (½ pt) whipped double cream. Pour into a container, cover and leave until just starting to set around the edge. Whisk well, return to the freezer and leave to re-set.

Adjust this basic recipe to create a variety of ice-creams. Omit the vanilla essence and flavour the custard with almond, fruit or coffee essence.

Add chocolate chips, chopped glacé fruits, dried fruit and nuts to give texture.

Add a few drops of food colouring if desired.

Serve the ice-cream with fresh or tinned fruit, wafer biscuits or meringues and top with a sauce.

See *Cakes, Fillings and Toppings* and *Sauces*

SOFTENING

Ice-cream can be softened in the microwave so that it is pliable enough to make bombes or set in moulds. Place 1 litre (1¾ pt) block of ice-cream in a bowl and microwave on Low (Defrost) for 1½–2 minutes. Chill moulds in the freezer before adding the ice-cream.

UNMOULDING

To loosen ice-cream from a mould or a container (not metal), microwave on Low (Defrost) for 15–30 seconds.

ICING

FONDANT

To make fondant icing more pliable and easier to use, wrap 225 g (8 oz) fondant in clingfilm and microwave on Low (Defrost) for 1–1½ minutes.

To melt fondant icing, place 225 g (8 oz) in a bowl and microwave on 100% High for 1½–2 minutes, stirring twice during cooking. Flavour or colour the icing if preferred. The icing will set on cooling.

Use to ice sponges or half dip fresh fruit, e.g. strawberries (leave hulls on), into the icing, then into chopped nuts. Leave to set. Serve as an after-dinner sweet.

ROYAL

Royal icing flowers and lattice patterns can be dried in the microwave on a Low (Defrost) or 10% setting. Do not microwave for longer than 15 seconds and leave to stand for 4-minute intervals.

INSULATING DISHES AND FOOD

Food cooked for a short time in the microwave cools quickly during standing time because the dish does not get hot and therefore cannot transfer heat to the food. Insulate dishes to assist in retaining heat in the food by placing them in a quilted holder, basket or by wrapping in napkins. They will also look more attractive on the table when serving.

To keep food hot during the standing time and to finish off the cooking process, cover or wrap in foil, shiny side in, so that the heat is reflected back into the food.

J

JAM

COOKING

Microwaved jam eliminates any condensation, odours and splattering.

Sugar added to the fruit must be dissolved before the jam has started to boil. To help this process, warm 450 g (1 lb) sugar on 50% Medium for 2 minutes. Use a 2.8 litre (5 pt) bowl for up to 1 kg (2 lb) fruit and stir regularly during the cooking time. A general rule is to use a container at least three times as large as the amount of ingredients being used.

QUANTITY

Do not make more than 1.8 kg (4 lb) jam at one time.

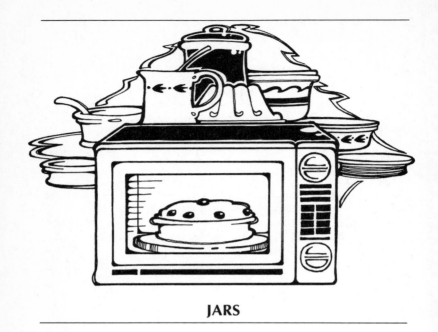

JARS

See *Sterilizing*

JELLY

DISSOLVING

Cut a packet of jelly into pieces or pull cubes apart. Place in a jug or bowl with 300 ml (½ pt) water. Microwave on 100% High for 1½–2 minutes, stirring once during cooking. Remove from the cooker and stir until the jelly has dissolved. Make up to 600 ml (1 pt) with ice-cubes and cold water. The jelly will then set in much less time.

UNMOULDING

To loosen made-up jellies from their moulds, microwave on Low (Defrost) for 30 seconds.

K

KEBABS

Always use wooden skewers and marinate the fish or meat kebabs for 2 hours to give more flavour, colour and tenderness to the food. Place four kebabs on a plate or prepared browning dish and brush with remaining marinade or a sauce of your choice. Cover with kitchen paper or greaseproof and microwave on 100% High for 3–4 minutes, then on Low (Defrost) for 10–12 minutes. Turn the kebabs regularly and baste with marinade during cooking.

Kebabs can also be microwaved on 50% Medium for 12–14 minutes if your cooker has a variable control.

Fish Kebabs can be cooked on 100% High for 4–6 minutes.

See *Marinades*

Remove the membrane encasing the kidney, cut in half and snip out the core using scissors. Kidneys can also be 'fried' like liver, using a browning dish. 450 g (1 lb) lamb's kidneys will take 8–10 minutes on 100% High. Turn and rearrange during cooking. Pig's and ox kidneys are tougher than lamb's, so require a lower power setting and longer cooking time.

KIDNEY BEANS

Do not attempt to cook kidney beans in the microwave as they should be boiled at a constant temperature by the conventional method to make them safe enough to eat.

KITCHEN PAPER

See *Covering Food*

L

LEEKS

Leeks cook well in a microwave. As so little water is used they keep their shape, colour and flavour well. Choose leeks of a uniform size so that they cook evenly. Trim the roots and tops of 450 g (1 lb) leeks, wash and place a single layer in a dish. Sprinkle with 4 tbsp water, cover and microwave on 100% High for 4–6 minutes, rearranging once during cooking. Stand for 3 minutes, drain and serve with white or cheese sauce.

See *Sauces*

LEMONS

See *Citrus, Curds*

LIMES

See *Citrus, Curds*

LIQUEURS

See *Wines and Liqueurs in Drinks*

LIQUIDS

Liquids should be heated in large, wide-necked jugs rather than tall, narrow jugs to reduce the risk of them boiling over.

Use conventional means when heating 600 ml (1 pt) or more of liquid as it will warm faster than using the microwave. This is important when adding stock, etc. to casseroles and soups as it will affect the cooking time.

LIVER

Liver cooks quickly and evenly in the microwave. There is less shrinkage and the meat remains moist. However, overcooking will toughen it, so timing is important. When cooked, the meat should be just pink when cut.

Slice the liver or prick with a fork to break the membrane. It can be 'fried' in the microwave using a browning dish. Cover with kitchen paper or greaseproof to prevent spitting. 450 g (1 lb) liver will take 6–8 minutes on 100% High. Reduce the timing by 2 minutes if using calf's liver as it has a more delicate texture.

LOW FAT SPREADS

Low fat spreads usually separate when used in conventional cookery but this does not happen when heated in the micro-wave. They are ideal to use as a glaze for food if you are calorie conscious. Use as a substitute for butter in flavoured butter, halving the microwave time when heating.

See *Butter, Flavoured*

M

MARGARINE

See *Butter*

MARINADES

Steep meat overnight or for a few hours in a marinade, if possible. It will add extra flavour, tenderize the meat and assist in browning, so making it more appealing.

Use marinades for steaks, chops, cutlets, chicken portions: generally any meats that are usually grilled.

Drain the meat and use the remaining marinade as a baste during cooking or thicken with cornflour and serve as an accompanying sauce.

BASIC

Combine equal quantities of vegetable oil and lemon juice. Add spices or herbs from the following: crushed black peppercorns, onion powder, crushed garlic cloves or powder, barbecue seasoning, lamb, pork or chicken seasoning, fresh or dried herbs, mustard, tomato sauce, Worcestershire sauce, soy sauce, ginger, sugar, vinegar etc.

BARBECUE

Mix 4 tbsp tomato sauce, 4 tbsp brown sauce, 2 tbsp Worcestershire sauce, 2 tbsp soft brown sugar, 1 tsp mustard. Use for chicken and pork.

LEMON

Mix 3 tbsp oil, 3 tbsp lemon juice, ½ tsp black pepper, 1 tbsp chopped fresh parsley. Use for fish.

WINE

Mix 150 ml (¼ pt) dry red wine, 3 tbsp oil, 3 tbsp red wine vinegar, 1 tsp thyme, 1 tbsp brown sugar. Use for lamb and beef.

MARMALADE

Cook marmalades in the microwave using the same basic principles of jam but remember the peel of citrus fruit takes longer to soften than jam-making fruit. To assist the softening, place chopped or shredded peel in a bowl with 150 ml (¼ pt) water. Cover and microwave on 100% High for 5–7 minutes. The softened peel may then be added to the other ingredients. Chop the pips and tie in a muslin bag to help release the pectin during microwaving. Remove when setting point is reached.

See *Jam*

MARROW

DICE

Marrow can be cooked in slices or dice without the addition of any water.

Place 450 g (1 lb) diced marrow in a dish. Cover and microwave on 100% for 6–8 minutes, tossing twice during cooking. Season and leave to stand for 2 minutes. Serve with a mild mustard or cheese sauce.

STUFFED

Place stuffed rings of sliced marrow in a casserole with 4 tbsp stock. Cover with pierced clingfilm and microwave on 100% High for 6–8 minutes. Rearrange the rings, turn the dish and baste once during cooking. Leave to stand for 2 minutes before serving with tomato sauce.

See *Sauce, Tomato*

MARZIPAN

To make marzipan more pliable and easier to use, wrap 225 g (8 oz) in clingfilm and microwave on Low (Defrost) for 1–1½ minutes.

MEAT

As a general rule, if the total cooking time is 15 minutes or more, a joint brushed with unsalted butter will brown naturally. It is best, however, to assist this process by brushing meat with a browning agent or glaze before microwaving. Seal meat under a grill or in a frying pan or cook in a roasting bag.

Cook joints of meat on an upturned saucer in a dish so juices can drain away. Do not add or sprinkle meat with salt before or during cooking as it dries it out (the exception being the crackling on pork).

Leave meat covered and at room temperature for 30–60 minutes before microwaving. Turn joints of meat frequently during cooking and leave to stand wrapped in foil, shiny side inwards, for 15–30 minutes before carving.

Place thicker parts of chops, etc. towards the outside of the dish, turn over and rotate the dish during cooking. When reheating sliced meat, add 1 tbsp stock or thin gravy per portion to help keep it moist and succulent.

See *Browning Agents, Casseroles, Chicken, Coatings, Duck, Meat Glazes and Bastes, Turkey*

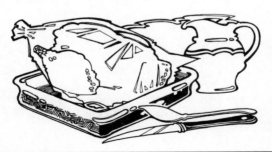

BASIC COOKING GUIDES FOR JOINTS

Baste joints of meat except pork during microwaving, unless cooking in a roasting bag. Timings are for 100% High or 50% Medium settings per 450 g (1 lb).

BEEF

	Minutes at 100% High	Minutes at 50% Medium	
TOPSIDE	5	10–11	rare
	6–7	11–13	medium
	8–9	14–16	well done
RIB	7	13–15	rare
	8–9	14–16	medium
	9–12	16–18	well done
RIB	6	11–12	rare
BONED and	7–8	13–15	medium
ROLLED	9–10	16–18	well done
SIRLOIN	5	10–11	rare
	6–7	11–13	medium
	8–9	14–16	well done

LAMB

LEG	8–9	10–12
BONED AND ROLLED	9–10	13–14
SHOULDER	9–10	13–14

PORK

Do not cover. Oil the skin and rub in salt. Leg and loin joints with the bone in should be microwaved on 100% High for the first 8 minutes, then on 50% Medium for 17–18 minutes per 450 g (1 lb).

Shoulder joints with the bone in – microwave on 100% High for the first 8 minutes, then on 50% Medium for 14–16 minutes per 450 g (1 lb).

BACON, GAMMON AND HAM JOINTS

Cook these joints in a roasting bag and follow the same basic rules as for cooking meat. It is best to cook bacon joints on a 50% Medium setting for 10–16 minutes per 450 g (1 lb), depending on the tenderness of the cut.

Wrap cooked joints in foil after microwaving and stand for 15–30 minutes to finish the cooking.

It is safest to use a temperature probe to test if joints of meat are cooked.

See *Temperature Probe*

MEAT GLAZES AND BASTES

Whenever possible, use unsalted butter in a baste as salt will toughen the food.

FOR BACON, GAMMON AND HAM

1.   3 tbsp clear honey mixed with the rind and juice of 1 orange and 1 tbsp soft brown sugar.
2.   1 small jar of cranberry jelly mixed with 4 tbsp cider vinegar.

FOR BEEF

Microwaved beef browns quite well without the assistance of a glaze. Use the drained meat juices to enhance a gravy or sauce.

FOR CHICKEN

1.   4 tbsp clear honey mixed with 1 tbsp sherry.

2.   Grated rind and juice of 1 lemon mixed with 1 tsp mustard and 1 tbsp brown sauce.

3.   4 tbsp tomato ketchup mixed with 2 tbsp brown sugar, 1 tsp mustard, 1 tsp Worcestershire sauce, 1 tbsp cider vinegar.

FOR DUCK

1. 4 tbsp marmalade mixed with 4 tbsp dry white wine.

2. 4 tbsp cranberry sauce or jelly mixed with 1 tbsp lemon juice and 3 tbsp dry red wine.

3. 4 tbsp apricot, peach, cherry or pineapple purée mixed with 2 tbsp sherry or port and 1 tbsp lemon juice.

FOR LAMB

1. 2 tbsp marmalade mixed with 2 tbsp clear honey, 2 tsp lemon juice, 2 tsp Worcestershire sauce.

2. 4 tbsp mint jelly mixed with 2 tbsp red wine vinegar, 2 tsp brown sugar.

3. 4 tbsp redcurrant jelly mixed with 3 tbsp sherry and 1 tbsp lemon juice.

FOR PORK

1. 4 tbsp clear honey mixed with 1 tbsp dry cider and 1 tsp chopped sage.

2. 4 tbsp barbecue sauce mixed with 1 tbsp clear honey and 1 tsp soy sauce.

3. 2 tbsp clear honey mixed with 4 tbsp dry cider and 1 tsp dried sage.

MERINGUES

Crisp, white meringues can be cooked in minutes in the microwave. Whisk one egg white until frothy and gradually mix in 350 g (12 oz) sifted icing sugar. When the mixture stiffens, knead by hand to form a ball. Divide in two and roll each piece into a long sausage. Cut both lengths into 24 pieces, roll these into balls and place 6 in a ring on a sheet of greaseproof paper. Microwave on 100% High for 1½–2 minutes until well risen, crisp and dry. Leave to stand for 5 minutes, remove paper and cool on a rack. Repeat with the remaining 42 pieces.

Store cooked meringues in an airtight container for up to three weeks.

The meringue mixture may be coloured if preferred and when cooked sandwiched together with fresh cream or dipped in chocolate. Knead 50 g (2 oz) desiccated coconut into the sugar dough for coconut meringues.

Conventional recipe meringue toppings can be microwaved (e.g. lemon meringue pie) but the result will be soft and white. Microwave on 100% High for 1½–2 minutes. Brown under a hot grill or sprinkle with coconut or brown sugar before microwaving. Decorate with cherries and angelica.

PAVLOVA

Roll half of the meringue mixture to a 16–18 cm (6–7 inch) circle on a sheet of greaseproof paper. Microwave on 100% High for 1½–2 minutes. When cold, decorate with fruit and cream.

MILK

Heat milk for cereals in a bowl by microwaving 150 ml (¼ pt) on 100% High for 20–30 seconds.

A cup or mug of hot milk will take 1½–2 minutes on 100% High.

See *Puddings, Milk*

MOISTURE

Whenever possible wrap moist and starchy foods in clingfilm to prevent evaporation, e.g. reheating jacket potatoes, corn on the cob, sweet or savoury puddings.

MOUSSE

To loosen mousses from their moulds microwave on Low (Defrost) for 30 seconds.

MUSHROOMS

Try to choose mushrooms of a uniform size so that they will cook evenly. Wash, pat dry and trim the stems. Do not peel the skins. Place 125 g (4 oz) mushrooms in a dish with 15 g (½ oz) butter and a squeeze of lemon juice. Cover and microwave on 100% High for 2–3 minutes, stirring halfway through cooking time. Stand for 1 minute before serving. Use any juices to flavour stocks, sauces and gravies.

STUFFED

To microwave 225 g (8 oz) stuffed mushrooms, wash, pat dry and remove stalks. Mound your favourite filling into the mushroom cap and arrange them on a plate lined with a sheet of kitchen paper. Microwave on 100% High for 3–4 minutes. Flat or large cap mushrooms are the best choice as the cavity is much larger than button.

MUSSELS

See *Shellfish*

N

NECTARINES

See *Fruit*

NUTS

ENHANCING FLAVOUR

Place 225 g (8 oz) salted peanuts in a dish and microwave on 100% High for 20–30 seconds.

REFRESHING

To re-crisp soft shelled nuts, heat on 100% High for ½–1 minute.

To re-crisp unshelled, plain roasted peanuts (monkey nuts), put 125 g (4 oz) nuts in a dish and place in the microwave. Cook uncovered on 100% High for 1½–2 minutes, tossing two or three times during cooking. Cool and shell.

ROASTING AND SALTING

Place 175 g (6 oz) shelled and husked nuts in a shallow dish with 1 tsp oil. Microwave on 100% High for 3–5 minutes or until lightly browned, tossing every minute. Lay on kitchen paper and cool. If salting, sprinkle over nuts and toss while still warm.

SHELLING

To make shelling easier, place 225 g (8 oz) Brazils, almonds, pecans, walnuts, hazelnuts (or an assortment) in a large bowl and pour over 225 ml (8 fl oz) water. Cover and microwave on 100% High for 3–4 minutes or until water boils. Stand for 1 minute, drain and spread on kitchen paper to cool. The nuts may then be cracked open, taking care because the shells may contain hot water.

SPICED

Mix 225 g (8 oz) peanuts with 1 tsp spice of your choice, e.g. curry, Worcestershire sauce, chilli, garlic, etc., and 15 g (½ oz) melted butter. Mix well and microwave uncovered on 100% High for 1½–2½ minutes, tossing two or three times during cooking. These are best served warm to enjoy their full flavour.

See *Almonds, Chestnuts, Hazelnuts*

O

ODOURS

Occasionally the microwave may need to be refreshed if strong smelling foods have been cooked, e.g. kippers or chutneys. Place 2 slices of lemon in a jug of hot water and microwave on 100% High for 2 minutes.

Remove the jug and wipe the inside of the cooker with a clean dry cloth.

ONIONS

Peel 450 g (1 lb) medium-sized onions. Place in a casserole, cover and microwave on 100% High for 8–10 minutes, re-arranging and turning the dish once during cooking. Sprinkle with salt and leave to stand for 2 minutes. Serve with a sour cream dressing or white sauce.

STUFFED

Stuffed onions can be cooked as above. Scoop out the centre and fill with stuffing. Add 4 tbsp stock and cover with pierced clingfilm. Baste the onions with stock twice during cooking. Leave to stand for 2 minutes before serving. Serve with tomato sauce.

See *Sauces*

ORANGES

See *Citrus, Curds*

P

PANCAKES

Batters cannot be cooked in the microwave. However, pancakes can be reheated. Loosely roll four cooked pancakes and arrange on a plate. Cover with clingfilm and microwave on 100% High for 40–60 seconds.

PARSNIPS

When microwaving parsnips add 1 tbsp lemon juice to the water before cooking to retain their white colour.

Prepare 450 g (1 lb) parsnips, turnips or swedes (or a combination) and place in a dish with 3 tbsp water. Cover and microwave on 100% High for 9–12 minutes, tossing twice during cooking. Stand for 3 minutes.

Season, drain and serve with cheese or lemon sauce. Swedes are best diced, cooked and mashed with a little butter and sprinkled with nutmeg.

DRIED

Place 225 g (8 oz) pasta in a deep dish and cover with boiling water, adding 1 tsp salt and 1 tbsp oil. Stir well and without covering microwave on 100% High for 5–6 minutes, stirring twice during cooking to prevent the pasta from sticking together. Stand covered for 5 minutes, then drain and serve for perfect pasta.

FRESH

Place 225 g (8 oz) fresh pasta in a deep dish. Cover with salted boiling water and microwave on 100% High for 2–3 minutes. Stir once during cooking.

PRE-COOKED PASTA

Cannelloni and lasagne that does not require pre-cooking can be used in your favourite recipe and microwaved successfully. Make the meat fillings more moist and increase the quantity of sauce slightly to give a thicker coating to the pasta. Only sprinkle the top of the food with cheese 2 minutes before the end of the cooking time otherwise it will be tough and stringy. A recipe using 8–10 cannelloni will take 8–10 minutes on 100% High. Brown under a hot grill or garnish with sliced tomato and sprinkle with chopped parsley. Use the same method for lasagne. Serve with garlic or herb French bread.

See *Bread, French*

PASTRY

COOKING

After cooking a pastry case, seal the pricked base by brushing with beaten egg yolk. Microwave on 100% High for 30–60 seconds or until yolk has set. This will prevent any filling, such as fruit and lemon meringue, seeping through to the pastry and making it soggy.

PASTRY SHAPES

Roll out any pastry trimmings and cut into small shapes to decorate desserts or serve with soups and casseroles. Microwave as for 'lids', adjusting the cooking time to suit the amount to be microwaved.

PUFF

Puff pastry cooks well in the microwave but watch it carefully as the inside browns while the outside is still pale. After rolling out, chill the pastry in the refrigerator for 30 minutes before cooking. When the pastry is cooked it should hold its shape and not flop when the oven door is opened. Lay a rectangle of rolled and prepared pastry on two sheets of kitchen paper and microwave on 100% High. 125 g (4 oz) will take 2–3 minutes.

SHORTCRUST BASES

Do not attempt to cook double-crust pies or filled flan cases in the microwave. The filling will cook before the pastry, making it wet and doughy.

Shortcrust pastry bases cook well on their own if a few basic rules are followed:

1. Do not add sugar to the pastry before cooking as it will burn.

2. Chill the pastry base in the refrigerator for 30 minutes before microwaving.

3. Use a mixture of brown and white flour to make the pastry.

4. Add a few drops of yellow food colouring to the mixture to improve the appearance.

5. Prick the base and sides of the pastry case well before cooking.

6. Line the base of the pastry case with two sheets of kitchen paper for the first half of the cooking time, to absorb moisture.

7. Do not attempt to cook a base larger than 23 cm (9 inch) in diameter.

8. Place the prepared flan dish on an upturned saucer in the microwave to assist in even cooking.

A 20–23 cm (8–9 inch) pastry base will take 4–5 minutes to cook on 100% High. Turn the dish every minute.

SHORTCRUST LIDS

To make a 'false' lid for a pie, roll pastry to 20 cm (8 inch) circle, prick well and chill. Place on a sheet of non-stick paper (not waxed) in the cooker and microwave on 100% High for 2–3 minutes until crisp and dry. Mark the pastry into sections before cooking if desired so that it can be portioned easily.

A dusting of paprika, microwave seasoning or sesame seeds before microwaving will improve the colour when cooked.

SHORTCRUST TARTLETS

Follow the same rules for pastry bases. Either use special microwave tartlet trays or mould small circles of pastry round upturned dishes or ramekins.

SUET

Suet pastry cannot be 'baked' using a microwave. It is only suitable for use in pudding and dumpling recipes, producing excellent results and reducing the cooking time to minutes.

See *Dumplings and Puddings*

REHEATING PIES

Cover pies loosely with kitchen paper to help retain a crisp pastry.

Sweet pie fillings become extremely hot when reheated due to the high sugar content, but the pastry remains cool. Leave them to stand after microwaving to equalize the temperature.

PÂTÉ

Pâtés cook beautifully in the microwave and the cooking time is considerably shorter than the conventional method. Most conventional recipes can be converted for the microwave, although the finished result may be slightly wetter than usual. Reduce the liquid content slightly in the recipe and adjust the seasonings, because they intensify with microwave cookery.

Try to cook pâtés in round dishes rather than oblong so that they cook more evenly. As a general rule, pâté using 450 g (1 lb) of pig's liver will take 7–10 minutes on 100% High. Cover the top of the pâté with greaseproof paper during cooking.

SOFTENING

To soften stiff pâtés for easier spreading, remove foil wrappings. Cover with clingfilm and microwave on Low (Defrost) for a few seconds.

PAVLOVA

See *Meringue*

PEACHES

See *Fruit*

PEARS

As pears discolour once peeled, brush with lemon juice before poaching in sugar syrup or poach in a red wine sugar syrup.

Place four peeled and cored pears in a deep dish and pour over sugar syrup, coating them well. Cover and microwave on 100% High for 5–7 minutes, turning the dish halfway through cooking. Stand for 3 minutes. Serve hot with cream or custard or leave to cool, turning the pears in the syrup at intervals to flavour and colour them evenly. Serve chilled with fresh cream.

See *Sugar Syrup, Fruit*

PEAS

MANGE TOUT

Mange tout peas are cooked to perfection in the microwave, retaining their colour and crispness well. Wash and drain 450 g (1 lb) mange tout and place in a bowl with 25 g (1 oz) butter. Cover and microwave on 100% High for 4–5 minutes, tossing twice during cooking. Season and stand for 2 minutes.

Serve with white sauce or toss with crisply fried bacon pieces.

PEPPERS

Prepare stuffed peppers and place in a deep casserole dish. Cover and microwave on 100% High for 5 minutes. Rearrange, turn dish and microwave for a further 5 minutes. Serve with tomato sauce.

The skins of microwaved peppers may be slightly tougher than when conventionally cooked, but time and flavour loss is reduced as they do not need to be blanched before cooking.

See *Sauces, Tomato*

PIES

See *Pastry*

PIZZAS

If fresh or frozen pizzas are microwaved on a prepared browning dish they will retain a crisp bottom and brown underneath. Do not slice a pizza on a browning dish as it could damage the surface.

Browning dishes are not essential when cooking pizzas. They can be cooked on any suitable dish or plate. If cooked on a roasting rack the dough will be drier as the steam can escape underneath. To give a fresh pizza dough base a crunchier crust, brush the plate with melted butter and sprinkle it with breadcrumbs, poppy seeds, or sesame seeds before placing the dough on it.

Microwave a 20 cm (8 inch) pizza on 100% High for 4–6 minutes. If cooking on a browning dish increase the cooking time by 1–2 minutes, checking to see that the bottom does not overcook. If possible top the pizza with grated cheese 2 minutes before the end of the cooking time so that it does not toughen and overcook.

DEEP DISH PIZZA

When making deep dish pizzas, press the prepared dough into a deep plate 20–24 cm (8–10 inch) in diameter and leave to rise for 30 minutes. Microwave on 100% High for 3–4 minutes until the base is dry but still spongy. Fill the pizza with cooked meat filling, sprinkle with cheese and microwave on 100% High for 2–3 minutes more. Sprinkle with chopped parsley after cooking.

QUICK PIZZA

Rub 175 g (6 oz) plain flour, 50 g (2 oz) margarine and 2 tsp mixed herbs together. Bind with 4 tbsp milk. Roll out to a 20 cm (8 inch) diameter and lay on a plate or a flat dish.

Mix together 75 g (3 oz) grated cheese, 50 g (2 oz) chopped ham or continental sausage and 2 tbsp tomato ketchup. Spread on the pizza base and microwave on 100% High for 2½–3½ minutes. Substitute half brown for white flour if wished. This pizza will have a crisper base if cooked on a browning dish and is best served cold with salad.

Use split muffins, French sticks, crumpets, rolls, melba toast, scones etc. to make snack pizzas in seconds. Just top them with a jar of ready prepared pizza topping, sprinkle with cheese and microwave on 100% High until hot and the cheese melted.

See *Scones, Dough*

PLUMS

See *Fruit, Poaching*

POPCORN

It is safest to use a specially designed corn popper to avoid any damage to the magnetron in the cooker.

CHOC FRUIT AND NUT

Add chopped nuts and cherries to cooked popcorn. Bind together with some melted chocolate. Spoon into paper cake cases and leave to set.

REHEATING

Place approximately 1 litre (2 pt) popped corn in a large bowl and microwave uncovered on 100% High for 1 minute until warm, tossing once.

For toffee-coated popcorn, heat 125 g (4 oz) sugar with 150 ml (¼ pt) water in a large bowl or jug and microwave on 100% High for 2 minutes, stirring twice during cooking. Make sure the sugar has completely dissolved and microwave the syrup on 100% High for a further 8–10 minutes until golden brown. Take care because the syrup is extremely hot. Pour over the popcorn and toss well to give a crispy coating.

SAVOURY

Season cooked popcorn while still warm with a sprinkling of salt, curry powder or paprika and serve with party drinks.

POPPADUMS

Place two or three poppadums on the cooker base and microwave on 100% High for 45–60 seconds until puffy. Cool on a rack for a few seconds before serving.

Poppadums may also be lightly brushed with oil on both sides. Microwave one for 20–25 seconds on 100% High, turning over once during cooking. Place on kitchen paper to cool before serving.

PORRIDGE

Porridge can be made easily in the serving dish with no sticky pan to wash. Place 120 g (8 tbsp) easy cook rolled oats in a bowl. Add a pinch of salt, 300 ml (½ pt) water or milk and water mixed and stir well. Microwave on 100% High for 3 minutes, stirring twice during cooking. Stand covered for 1 minute, stir well and serve with sugar, honey or syrup.

SCOTTISH

To make a traditional Scottish porridge, use medium or coarse oatmeal instead of rolled oats.

Place 90 g (6 tbsp) oatmeal in a bowl. Add a pinch of salt, 450 ml (¾ pt) water or milk and water mixed and stir well. Microwave on 100% High for 4–6 minutes, stirring twice during cooking. Stand covered for 1 minute, stir well and serve with soft brown sugar and a topping of cream.

POTATOES

CHIPS

Oven chips may be cooked on a browning dish in the microwave with excellent results. Prepare the dish to the manufacturer's instructions and coat lightly with oil. Cook two portions of chips on 100% High for 3–5 minutes, tossing two or three times during cooking.

DICED

Cook diced potatoes for use in salads. Place 225 g (8 oz) diced potatoes (skins left on) in a dish with 1 tbsp water. Cover and microwave for 2–3 minutes. Toss and microwave for a further 2–3 minutes. Leave to stand for 2 minutes. Cool and add to salad recipes or serve with a salad dressing or mayonnaise.

JACKET

Wash and pierce the skin of a 125–175 g (4–6 oz) potato. Place on a piece of kitchen paper inside the cooker and microwave on 100% High for 4–6 minutes, turning over halfway through cooking time.

Jacket potatoes will stay piping hot for half an hour if wrapped in foil after cooking. (Do *not* reheat in foil.)

Reheat jacket potatoes by wrapping securely in clingfilm. Microwave on 100% High for 30–45 seconds for each potato and they will taste freshly cooked.

NEW

A few drops of lemon juice added to the water before cooking new potatoes will prevent them from turning black around the edges. Pierce the skins or score round the centre before cooking to prevent the skins from bursting.

POULTRY

Brush uncooked poultry with melted butter or margarine and sprinkle with colour enhancers (see *Browning Agents*). Place in a pierced roasting bag on a dish and microwave on 100% High for 6 minutes per 450 g (1 lb). Cook whole large birds upside down on each side before turning breast uppermost to ensure even cooking.

See *Chicken*

PRAWNS

See *Shellfish*

PRESERVES

See *Citrus, Curds, Jam, Marmalade*

PRUNES

It is not necessary to pre-soak prunes when cooked in the microwave. Place 225 g (8 oz) prunes in a dish with enough water or cold tea to cover them. Cover and microwave on 100% High for 4–5 minutes, stirring once during cooking. Stand for 5 minutes to plump up before serving.

PUDDINGS

When microwaving suet and sponge puddings, remove clingfilm covering as soon as they are cooked so that it does not contract and squash them. Microwaved puddings are much lighter in texture and rise more than when conventionally cooked, but they tend to dry out much quicker. They can be refreshed once by reheating if eaten immediately.

When reheating steamed puddings, moisture may easily be lost. For best results, arrange a single layer of slices round the edge of a plate, placing a glass of water in the centre. Cover loosely with clingfilm. Microwave on 100% High for 1–2½ minutes or until the underside of the plate feels warm to touch. Slices may also be wrapped individually in clingfilm and warmed as above without the water.

MILK

As a general rule, use 50 g (2 oz) grain, e.g. rice, semolina, tapioca, to 600 ml (1 pt) liquid and 2 tbsp sugar. Cook on 50% Medium power to reduce the risk of boiling over.

RICE

Rice puddings can be made in the microwave, but will not have a brown skin on the surface. They are creamier than when conventionally cooked and the texture slightly thicker. To assist in softening the grains of rice for a creamier pudding, soak them in the cooking liquid overnight.

Place 50 g (2 oz) short grain rice in a large bowl with 600 ml (1 pt) milk and 2 tbsp sugar. Cover and microwave on 100% High for 4–5 minutes until boiling, stirring once. Reduce to 50% Medium and microwave for a further 30–35 minutes, stirring twice during cooking. Stand for 5 minutes. Stir well and serve.

Substitute 150 ml (¼ pt) of the milk with evaporated or condensed milk for a richer pudding. If using condensed milk, omit the sugar.

Add cinnamon, mixed spice, lemon or orange zest, vanilla sugar for a flavoured pudding.

Add chopped, dried fruit, sultanas or nuts to the pudding halfway through cooking time for a more interesting pudding.

Most grain puddings can be made using this method.

SPONGE

Do not microwave sponge pudding recipes that use a covering of syrup, honey, jam, or high sugar content ingredient in the bottom of the basin. Microwave energy is attracted to sugars causing them to burn with prolonged heating.

When making a pudding using a fresh fruit base, microwave on medium power to stop moisture being drawn from the fruit and making the sponge wet and soggy.

A layer of breadcrumbs sprinkled over fruit or liquid in the bottom of the pudding will absorb moisture and prevent it being soggy. Add up to 1 tbsp more liquid to sponge pudding recipes when cooking in the microwave. Only half fill the basin with mixture and cover loosely with vented clingfilm. A 125 g (4 oz) sponge mixture will take 4–6 minutes on 100% High to cook.

Microwaved puddings sometimes look undercooked and soft on the top. To check if they are done, leave to stand for 5 minutes and test with a skewer. Return to the cooker for a few seconds more if they are undercooked. Prepare dishes and basins as for cakes.

SUET

Suet puddings cook extremely well in the microwave. They are lighter in texture than when conventionally cooked, but the greatest advantage is that they cook in minutes without filling the kitchen with condensation.

Improve the appearance of a sweet pudding by sprinkling toasted breadcrumbs or biscuit crumbs inside the basin before cooking. Loosely cover the surface of a pudding before cooking with vented clingfilm to assist in retaining the moisture. Never fill to the top of the basin and leave at least 2.5 cm (1 inch) to allow for the pudding to rise. Stand for 5 minutes before serving. A suet pudding should be well risen and puffy, and the top appear flaky when cooked.

Layers of fruit and suet pastry placed in a pudding basin produce very good results when cooked. A 225 g (8 oz) recipe will take 6–8 minutes on 100% High to cook.

To microwave a jam roll using 225 g (8 oz) suet pastry, place the roll seam down on a sheet of lightly greased greaseproof paper and microwave on 100% high for 4–5 minutes. Brown under a grill and sprinkle with sugar to serve.

See *Dumplings, Sauces*

YORKSHIRE PUDDING

Yorkshire puddings cannot be made in a microwave but they can be reheated. Place four cooked Yorkshires in a circle on a sheet of kitchen paper. Microwave on 100% High for 20–30 seconds.

PULSES

It is better to cook pulses by the conventional method as there is hardly any timesaving and often the outer covering of the pulses burst during microwaving.

See *Kidney Beans*

Q

QUICHE

Quiche can be cooked successfully in the microwave, if a 50% Medium power setting is used.

Microwave a 20 cm (8 inch) pastry case and fill with ingredients of your choice. Beat the eggs, milk and seasonings together and pour over the filling. Microwave for 15–20 minutes on 50% Medium, turning the dish four times during cooking. Stand for 5 minutes and brown the top under a hot grill to improve the appearance.

See *Pastry*

R

RATATOUILLE

Ratatouille is easily made in the microwave as the vegetables can cook in their own juices if preferred. Microwave the onions and butter for 1½–2 minutes before adding the other ingredients and cook in a covered dish for 8–10 minutes, stirring twice during cooking. Season and leave to stand for 3–4 minutes before serving.

Garnish with parsley and serve hot as a vegetable or leave to cool, chill in the refrigerator and serve as a salad.

RICE

There is no time saved when cooking rice in the microwave, but it results in fluffy, separate grains.

For salads, cool the rice and add salad dressings. Garnish with lemon wedges and parsley. Serve chilled.

Brown or white rice may be flavoured with tomato purée, curry paste, herbs or add cooked vegetables, sultanas, cheese, etc. for a more interesting variation.

To cook 175 g (6 oz) long grain rice, place in a large casserole with 400 ml (14 fl oz) boiling salted water. Cover with a loose lid and microwave on 100% High for 12–14 minutes, stirring once during cooking. Stand for 3 minutes. All the liquid will be absorbed and the rice just needs fluffing up with a fork before serving.

BROWN RICE

To cook 175 g (6 oz) brown rice use the method above but microwave for 20–25 minutes. Stand for 3 minutes, fluff up and use as required.

If your microwave has a variable control, cook the rice for 2–3 minutes on 100% High, then reduce to 50% Medium. Add 5–10 minutes to the timings if using this method. Microwaving the rice on a medium setting will reduce the risk of the water boiling over.

REHEATING

Rice can be reheated successfully too: place two portions of cooked rice in a covered dish and microwave on 100% High for 2–3 minutes. Toss well to separate the grains and serve.

See *Puddings*

ROASTING BAGS

See *Covering Food*

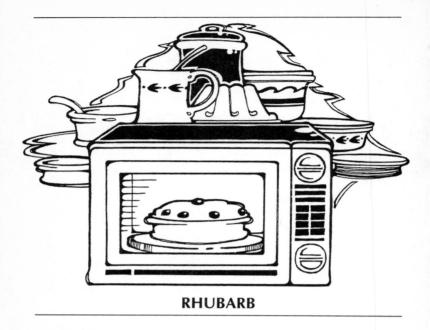

RHUBARB

BLANCHING

Prepare 450 g (1 lb) as for cooking (below) and microwave on 100% High for 2–3 minutes, tossing halfway through cooking time.

COOKING

There is no mushy result when cooked in the microwave. Cut 350 g (12 oz) washed rhubarb into 2.5 cm (1 inch) pieces and place in a dish with 2 tbsp water. Cover loosely and microwave on 100% High for 5–6 minutes, tossing halfway through cooking time. Stir in 125 g (4 oz) sugar and 1 tsp lemon juice. Stand covered for 3 minutes before serving.

ROLLS

See *Bread*

S

SAFETY

Never switch on a microwave when it is empty as it could damage the components.

Keep a cup of water inside the cooker to prevent this happening.

SALT

DRYING

To dry damp salt, place in a bowl and microwave on 100% High for 20–40 seconds.

SEASONING

Season food with salt after it has been microwaved as it can toughen and dry out some foods if added before.

SAUCES

Sauces can be made in advance and reheated (covered) when required. This is a great advantage if entertaining as they can be warmed in the serving dish. For a speedy sauce, heat a tin of condensed soup.

BASIC WHITE

Melt 25 g (1 oz) butter, stir in 25 g (1 oz) plain flour and blend in 300 ml (½ pt) milk. Microwave on 100% High for 3–4 minutes, whisking twice during cooking. Season with salt and pepper. Serve with vegetables or fish.

The sauce can be enriched when cooked by adding 15–25 g (½–1 oz) butter or 4 tbsp cream, or beating in 1 egg yolk (make sure the sauce is not boiling). Alternatively, add one of the following:

Cheese   Add 75–125 g (3–4 oz) to the basic sauce. Heat for a few seconds if necessary to melt the cheese.

Egg   Add 2 chopped, hard-boiled eggs.

Mushroom   Add 50 g (2 oz) sliced cooked mushrooms.

Onion   Add 1 chopped and cooked onion.

Parsley   Add 2 tbsp chopped parsley.

Prawn   Add 50 g (2 oz) prawns and 1 tsp lemon juice.

BREAD

Mix half a grated onion, 50 g (2 oz) fresh breadcrumbs, 25 g (1 oz) butter, 150 ml (¼ pt) milk, 1 bay leaf, pinch of nutmeg, salt and pepper, in a bowl. Microwave on 50% Medium for 3–4 minutes, stirring halfway through cooking time. Remove bay leaf, stir well and serve. The sauce may be flavoured with clove instead of nutmeg.

CRANBERRY

Place 250 g (8 oz) cranberries, 150 ml (¼ pt) water, 175 g (6 oz) granulated sugar, 1 tsp lemon juice and the grated rind of half a lemon in a bowl. Mix well, cover and microwave on 100% High for 6–8 minutes. Stir and crush the cranberries two or three times during cooking. Then microwave on Low (Defrost) for a further 6–8 minutes, stirring and crushing as before. Cover and leave to cool to thicken the sauce. Serve with chicken, turkey or gammon.

TOMATO

Place 25 g (1 oz) butter, 1 chopped small red or green pepper and 1 small onion in a bowl. Cover and microwave on 100% High for 2 minutes, stirring once during cooking. Add 1 x 439 g (15 oz) tin of chopped tomatoes, 3 tbsp tomato purée, 2 tsp brown sugar, ½ tsp thyme and ½ tsp oregano. Mix well and microwave uncovered on 100% High for 3–4 minutes.

If a thinner sauce is required add a little stock. Liquidize the sauce if preferred.

Serve with stuffed peppers, aubergines, courgettes, onions and marrow.

SWEET SAUCES

ARROWROOT

An arrowroot sauce can be made quickly in the microwave and used to put a glaze on fruit flans or serve with ice-creams and sponge puddings. Blend 4 tsp arrowroot with 2 tbsp water. Microwave 300 ml (½ pt) canned fruit juice or pure fruit juice (top up with water if necessary) on 100% High for 2–3 minutes until just starting to boil. Pour on to arrowroot mixture and stir well. Microwave on 100% High for ½–1 minute until thick, stirring twice during cooking. Add sugar to sweeten if needed. The sauce may be flavoured with orange or lemon juice and add a few drops of colouring to improve its colour. Cool before glazing flans.

CARAMEL

Place 225 g (8 oz) caramel sweets and 6 tbsp milk in a bowl.

Microwave on 50% Medium for 2–3 minutes until the caramel has melted. Stir four times during cooking. Serve with sponge puddings or ice-cream.

CHERRY AND ALMOND

Place 50 g (2 oz) unsalted butter and 4 tbsp golden syrup in a bowl. Cover and microwave on 100% High for 1–1½ minutes until melted and hot. Add 50 g (2 oz) flaked almonds and 50 g (2 oz) chopped glacé cherries. Stir well and serve with sponge and suet puddings.

CLEAR LEMON OR ORANGE

Place 2 tsp cornflour, 125 g (4 oz) sugar, 50 g (2 oz) unsalted butter and the grated rind and juice of 1 orange or lemon in a bowl. Mix in 300 ml (½ pt) water and microwave on 100% High for 2–2½ minutes, whisking twice during cooking. Cook for a further 1½–2 minutes and whisk again.

FRUIT

To make delicious sauces for puddings and ice-creams, use canned fruit syrup made up to 300 ml (½ pt) with water. Blend in 1 tbsp cornflour and microwave on 100% High for 3–4 minutes, whisking halfway during cooking. And a few drops of colouring to improve the appearance if pale juices are used.

JAM

Heat jam in a jug on 100% High for a few seconds to make measuring and pouring sauces easier.

For a thinner jam sauce use equal quantities of jam and water with a few drops of lemon. Microwave on 100% High for 1 minute, stirring once during cooking.

MARSHMALLOW

Place 125 g (4 oz) marshmallows and 2 tbsp evaporated milk in a bowl and microwave on 50% Medium for 1½–2 minutes. Stir well and serve hot with ice-cream. Flavour the sauce with coffee, chocolate or essence.

QUICK CHOCOLATE

Place 125 g (4 oz) white, milk or plain chocolate in a bowl with 15 g (½ oz) butter, 2 tbsp water, 2 tbsp golden syrup. Microwave on 100% High for 2–3 minutes. This sauce will thicken on cooling. Serve hot with ice-cream or choux pastries. For variations use a flavoured chocolate, e.g. orange, or replace the water with brandy or rum.

SWEET WHITE

Place 15 g (½ oz) cornflour, 15 g (½ oz) butter and 1 tbsp caster sugar in a bowl. Blend in 300 ml (½ pt) milk and microwave on 100% High for 2–2½ minutes, whisking twice during cooking. Cook for a further 1½–2 minutes. Whisk again and flavour with vanilla, almond, brandy or rum essences, melted chocolate or coffee. Serve with sponge and suet puddings.

See *Cakes, Fillings and Toppings*

SAUSAGES

Sausages can be cooked in the microwave but will not colour without using a browning dish.

Prick the skins to break the membrane and prevent them from bursting. Brush 450 g (1 lb) sausages with a browning agent and place on a shallow dish lined with kitchen paper. Place another sheet on the top to absorb any spitting and microwave on 100% High for 5–6 minutes, rearranging once during cooking.

To make sausages look more appetizing, wrap a rasher of streaky bacon round each sausage before cooking and microwave.

CONTINENTAL

Boiling sausage rings can be microwaved in their plastic packaging. Pierce the bag and skin of an 225 g (8 oz) sausage. Place in a dish and microwave on 100% High for 1–1½ minutes. Turn the sausage over and cook for a further 1½ minutes. Stand for 2 minutes before serving.

SCONES

Scones can be cooked successfully in the microwave but tend to dry out more quickly than when conventionally cooked, so are best eaten when they are fresh and warm. As scones will not brown in the microwave, brush the tops with melted butter before cooking and sprinkle with breadcrumbs, biscuit crumbs, oats, spice, or brown under a hot grill after cooking. Add dried fruit and spices to the ingredients or a mixture of brown and white flour.

COOKING

To microwave eight scones, place in a circle on a sheet of greaseproof paper or shallow dish. Microwave on 100% High for 4–5 minutes until risen and springy when touched. Serve warm, split and buttered with jam or syrup.

Scones can be cooked on a browning dish and will look more appealing. Omit sprinkling the tops with breadcrumbs but still brush with butter before cooking. Prepare the browning dish, brush with oil and place the scones on it. Microwave on 100% High for 1½–2 minutes. Turn the scones over and microwave for a further 1½–2 minutes. Cool and dust with icing sugar.

SAVOURY

Add grated cheese, herbs, savoury spice, mustard, chopped bacon etc. to a basic savoury scone mixture and cook as before. Sprinkle the tops of the scones with the same ingredients before microwaving to improve their appearance. If using cheese as a topping, sprinkle over the scones halfway through cooking.

Scone dough can also be used as a pizza base and cooked successfully in the microwave. Microwave a 20 cm (8 inch) base on 100% High for 2 minutes. Arrange slices of ham, tomato, olives, etc. on the top and sprinkle with herbs and grated cheese. Microwave on 100% High until the cheese starts to melt.

SEASONINGS

Microwaving food intensifies all flavours, so use seasonings, herbs and spices very carefully, reducing the quantity when using conventional recipes for microwave cookery.

SESAME SEEDS

Toast sesame seeds by placing a few tablespoons in a shallow dish. Microwave on 100% High, tossing several times during cooking until golden brown. Use to decorate breads, vegetables, pastry dishes, etc.

SHELLFISH

Microwave energy is able to pass through the outer casing of shellfish as they do a covered dish. Because of this the full flavour of shellfish is appreciated.

MUSSELS

Cook and eat mussels on the day of purchase. Discard any

before cooking if their shells are open and will not close when tapped.

Scrub the mussels, remove any barnacles with a knife and pull away the beards. Place 450 g (1 lb) mussels, 15 g (½ oz) butter, 150 ml (¼ pt) dry white wine, 1 small onion, finely chopped, 1 garlic clove, crushed, and 1 tbsp chopped parsley in a bowl.

Cover and microwave on 100% High for approximately 3 minutes until the shells begin to open. Stir halfway through cooking time. Serve immediately with the juices and a sprinkling of fresh parsley. Mop up the liquor with warm crusty bread.

PRAWNS

Place 450 g (1 lb) fresh unpeeled prawns in a dish with 600 ml (1 pt) water, 2 bay leaves, salt and pepper. Cover and microwave on 100% High for 6–8 minutes until boiling. Stir halfway through cooking time. Stand for 1–2 minutes, then drain and cool. To reduce the fishy smell during cooking, add 1 tbsp vinegar to the water.

SHRIMPS

Use the method above, but microwave for 5–7 minutes.

SHORTBREAD

Shortbread can be made in the microwave but will not give as good a result than when conventionally cooked. Cream 100 g (4 oz) butter with 50 g (2 oz) caster sugar. Add 175 g (6 oz) plain flour and mix to form a soft dough. Press into a lightly greased 18–20 cm (7–8 inch) shallow dish. Prick the base well and pinch the edges with finger and thumb. Microwave on 100% High for 4–5 minutes. Leave to cool slightly, mark into triangles and sprinkle with sugar. Serve with mousses and fools or eat as a biscuit.

SHRIMPS

See *Shellfish*

SKIN

Prick, score or cut all foods that are enclosed in a skin or membrane before microwaving, e.g. tomatoes, potatoes, apples, liver, kidneys, fish, eggs, etc. Failure to do this will cause them to burst.

SOUP

When making conventional soup recipes in the microwave, remember to reduce the cooking liquid by up to half as there is less evaporation. Do not overseason as seasonings are intensified. Add hot stock or liquid to reduce the cooking time. Place the ingredients in a deep casserole to avoid boiling over, cover and cook on 100% High. Stir occasionally during cooking. Serve soup with flavoured French bread, croûtons or dumplings.

Pour a can of soup into a mug or bowl, cover and microwave on 100% High for 2–3 minutes. Stir once during cooking.

See *Bread, French, Croûtons* and *Dumplings*

SPAGHETTI

See *Pasta*

SPEEDY SNACKS

HAMBURGERS

Microwave one 125 g (4 oz) hamburger on 100% High for 1 minute each side. Stand for 1 minute and serve in a warmed bun with relish or mustard.

HOT DOG ROLLS

Prick four hot dog sausages and place in soft rolls. Wrap in kitchen paper and microwave on 100% High for 1½–2½ minutes. Serve with relish, ketchup, mustard, or fried onions.

HOT FILLED ROLLS

Fill four crusty rolls with filling of choice, wrap in kitchen paper
and microwave as before. Serve with coleslaw and salad.
See *Bread, Toasted sandwiches and Pitta bread*, and *Croissants*

SPICES

To avoid spices having a raw taste especially when using them in
foreign recipes, microwave with a little oil on 100% High for a
few seconds before adding them to the other ingredients.

See *Seasonings*

SPINACH

The microwave cooks spinach well. As no added water is used
most of the nutrients and vitamins are retained.
   Wash 450 g (1 lb) spinach and drain well. Place whole or
chopped leaves in a pierced boiling or roasting bag with a knob
of butter. Microwave on 100% High for 6–8 minutes, tossing
once during cooking. Season, toss again and leave to stand for 2
minutes. Spinach may also be cooked in a covered dish using
the same method.

SPRING GREENS

Wash, drain and cut away stalks. Shred the leaves and microwave as for spinach above.

STANDING TIME

Standing time is an important factor of microwave cookery,
because food continues to cook during that period. Generally

allow one third of the cooking time when leaving food to stand, but denser food will take longer. If cooking more than one food, e.g. jacket potatoes, the standing time need not be increased as this is catered for in the cooking time.

See *Foil*

STERILIZING

Sterilize jars to use for preserving by putting 150 ml (¼ pt) water into each jar. Microwave on 100% High until boiling and continue to heat for 1 minute. Remove the jars using oven gloves, pour out water and place open end down on kitchen paper. The hot jars can then be filled with preserves. Do not use this method for sterilizing babies' bottles and teats.

STIR-FRY

Stir-fry recipes work very well in the microwave. The cooking time is roughly the same as the conventional method, but smells are cut to a minimum, less stirring is required and the vegetables retain their colour, crispness and flavour.

Meat can be added to the vegetables, but ensure that all ingredients are cut to a uniform size to assist in even cooking. Cook the stir-fry in a browning dish for a slightly better result.

Microwave a vegetable stir-fry recipe uncovered for 4 servings on 100% High for 4–6 minutes, stirring twice during cooking. Microwave strips of meat on 100% High for 2–3 minutes, then continue as above when cooking meat stir-frys.

STOCKS

Use hot water when making stocks in the microwave. Place the ingredients in a deep casserole to avoid boiling over and cover with a lid to prevent evaporation.

Fish stock – microwave on 100% High for 8–10 minutes.
Meat bone – microwave on 100% High for 30–40 minutes.
Poultry – microwave on 100% High for 15–20 minutes.

STUFFINGS

BACON

Place 25 g (1 oz) butter in a bowl with 50 g (2 oz) chopped bacon, 1 chopped onion, 1 finely chopped carrot and microwave covered on 100% High for 2 minutes, stirring once halfway through cooking time. Add salt and pepper, 1 tsp chopped parsley and 50 g (2 oz) fresh breadcrumbs. Mix well and use to stuff chicken, lamb and pork joints.

RICE

Mix together 125 g (4 oz) cooked long grain rice, 1 chopped cooked onion, 50 g (2 oz) chopped cooked mushrooms, salt and pepper, 1 tsp dried herbs. Use to stuff vegetables, e.g. marrow, aubergines, peppers, onions.

SUGAR

DRYING

To dry damp sugar, place 125 g (4 oz) in a bowl and microwave on 100% High for 20–40 seconds.

SOFTENING

To soften brown sugar which has gone hard, place 225 g (8 oz) in a boiling bag and sprinkle with water or add a slice of apple. Tie loosely and microwave on 100% High for 30 seconds. Check halfway through cooking time. Leave to stand for 5 minutes before use.

SYRUP

Sugar syrups are basically used for poaching fresh fruits.

To make a light syrup, place 125 g (4 oz) sugar and 300 ml (½ pt) water in a bowl and microwave on 100% High for approximately 4 minutes until boiling. Stir every minute during cooking to ensure that the sugar dissolves.

Light syrup is suitable for poaching the 'sweeter' fruits, e.g. peaches, plums, nectarines, apricots, greengages, etc.

A heavier syrup may be required for poaching the 'tart' fruits, e.g. rhubarb, cooking apples, gooseberries. Use the same method as above, but increase the sugar to 175 g (6 oz).

A sugar syrup may be flavoured and coloured to improve the appearance and taste of the fruit when it is poached:

Red wine   Substitute red wine for water when making a light syrup. A dash of lemon juice will improve the flavour. This syrup is particularly good for poaching pears as they turn a rich red colour.

Spiced   Add a cinnamon stick and a few cloves. Strain the juice before using to poach apples.

SYRUP SAUCE, LIQUEUR

Make a light syrup sauce, reducing the water by 2 tbsp. Add 2 tbsp liqueur to the hot sauce and serve or use as required. The sauce may be coloured to improve its appearance.

Amaretto   Serve with peaches, nectarines, apricots, greengages. Decorate with ratafia biscuits or flaked biscuits.

Orange liqueur or Curaçao   Serve with pineapple, oranges, apricots, peaches.

Cherry brandy   Serve with red or black cherries, raspberries, pineapple, plums.

Apricot brandy   Serve with oranges, apricots, peaches.

Kirsch   Serve with red or black cherries, pineapple, greengages.

SYRUP SAUCE, SPIRIT

Spirits may also be used to flavour a light syrup sauce.

Brandy Serve with oranges, apricots, peaches, bananas.

Dark or white rum Serve with oranges, pears, bananas.

Vodka Serve with raspberries, pears, pineapple, greengages.

SWEETCORN

Place two corn on the cob in a dish with 4 tbsp water and a knob of butter. Cover and microwave on 100% High for 6–8 minutes, turning over halfway through cooking time. Leave to stand for 1 minute. To reheat whole sweetcorn, wrap securely in clingfilm and microwave one cob for 45–60 seconds to taste as good as freshly cooked.

SWEDES

See *Parsnips*

SYRUP

CRYSTALLIZED

To heat crystallized syrup, remove the metal lid from the jar and microwave on 50% Medium or Low (Defrost) for a few seconds to regain a smooth liquid.

MEASURING

Heat syrup in a jug for a few seconds on 100% High to make measuring easier.

See *Sugar*

T

TEA

A cup or mug of tea may be reheated in the microwave from cold and the flavour will not be affected. Heat on 100% High for 1½–2 minutes.

TEABREADS

See *Bread, Defrosting*

TEMPERATURE PROBE

A temperature probe is a specially designed thermometer for use in a microwave cooker. It determines the internal temperature of food, which is particularly useful when cooking joints of meat to test if they are cooked. Follow the manufacturer's instructions for their use.

Never use conventional meat or sugar thermometers in a microwave.

TOAST

To reheat cold buttered toast, place one slice on a sheet of kitchen paper and microwave on 100% High for 15 seconds.

TOMATOES

COOKING

To microwave four whole tomatoes, cut a small cross on the

base of the fruit and place in a dish stalk end down. Cover loosely with clingfilm and microwave on 100% High for 2–2½ minutes. Stand for 1 minute before serving.

PEELING

To peel easily, prick the skins of 1 kg (2 lb) tomatoes, place in a bowl and cover with boiling water. Microwave on 100% High for 30 seconds or until the skins begin to shrink from the flesh. Drain, cover with cold water and leave for 1 minute before skinning.

TURKEY

Follow the same basic rules as preparing and cooking chicken, but only stuff the neck and never the body cavity. Make sure there is at least a 5 cm (2 inch) gap between the turkey and the walls of the cooker. Microwave on 100% High for 9–11 minutes per 450 g (1 lb) or 11–13 minutes on 50% Medium. Stand in foil, shiny side inwards, for 30 minutes before carving. Serve with bread or cranberry sauce.

See *Chicken, Sauces*

TURNIPS

See *Parsnips*

U

UTENSILS

Do not leave metal spoons, forks, whisks, foil, etc. in the cooker when the microwave is in use.

Wooden spoons can be left in the microwave when making sauces or custards for short periods of time.

See *Dishes*

V

VEGETABLES

BLANCHING

Prepare 450 g (1 lb) washed and drained vegetables and place in a dish with 3 tbsp water. Cover and microwave on 100% High for 3 minutes, tossing halfway through cooking time. Place in a bowl of iced water until cold. Drain well and open freeze.

COOKING

Small quantities of frozen vegetables can be cooked in a freezer bag. Pierce the bag of a 225 g (8 oz) packet, place on a sheet of kitchen paper and microwave as usual.

Frozen vegetables may also be cooked in a serving dish, so reducing washing up.

MATCHSTICK

For a variation in cooking vegetables, cut them into match-stick-sized pieces 7.5 cm (3 inch) long.

To cook four servings, place 25 g (1 oz) butter in a dish and microwave on 100% High for 30 seconds, until melted. Add 225 g (8 oz) matchstick vegetables, cover and microwave on 100% High for 5–6 minutes, tossing once during cooking.

Season and leave to stand for 2 minutes before serving. Garnish with chopped parsley.

For speed, use a potato peeler to slice the vegetables instead of cutting into matchsticks.

REHEATING

Vegetables will reheat more quickly if covered with pierced clingfilm or a lid to retain their moisture.

See *individual vegetables, Stir-fry*

VINEGAR

FLAVOURED

Place a sprig of fresh herbs of your choice in a bottle or jar e.g. mint, tarragon, thyme or a mixture. Cover with 300–600 ml (½–1 pt) distilled malt vinegar and microwave on 100% High for ½–1½ minutes until just warm. Check regularly. Seal with a plastic lid and store in a cool, dark place for two weeks before using.

After opening, store in a refrigerator for up to eight weeks. Garlic and onion can also be used as flavourings, and cider vinegar instead of malt. Use when making marinades, salad dressings or mayonnaise.

W

WATER

See *Liquids*

WINE

Bring cold wine to room temperature by pouring into a large jug or heatproof carafe and microwave on 100% High for a few seconds.

MULLED

Pour 1 litre (1¾ pt) wine into a bowl. Add 125 g (4 oz) soft brown sugar, 6 cloves, 3 cinnamon sticks, pinch of mixed spice, 1 sliced orange and 1 sliced lemon. Mix well and microwave on 100% High for 5–7 minutes, stirring halfway through cooking to ensure the sugar is completely dissolved. Add a spirit of your choice after microwaving and strain if preferred.

WINE AND LIQUEURS IN DRINKS

When heating a drink containing alcohol, cover with pierced clingfilm to prevent excess evaporation and do not allow it to reach boiling point.

See *Flambéeing*

Y

YORKSHIRE PUDDINGS

See *Puddings*

Z

ZEST

See *Citrus, Zest*

NOTES

NOTES

NOTES

Opening doors to the World of books

Book Tokens

Book Tokens can be bought and exchanged at most bookshops